The Crowdfunding Playbook For Creators

Plan, Launch, And Fund Your Projects With Crowdfunding Sites

ETHAN.J.CODE

COPYRIGHT

DISCLAIMER

This book is designed to provide information. Every effort has been made to make this book as complete and accurate as possible, but no warranty or fitness is implied. The information is provided on an "as is" basis. The author and the publisher shall have neither liability nor responsibility to any person or entity with respect to any loss or damages arising from the information contained in this book or from the use of the programs accompanying it. This book contains examples of code and techniques that are provided for instructional purposes. While the author has made every attempt to ensure the accuracy and quality of the code, it should not be used as-is in professional or production environments without thorough testing and verification. The views expressed in this book are those of the author and do not necessarily reflect the views of any company or organization.

Table Of Contents

Chapter 1: The Crowdfunding Revolution: Beyond the Dollar Signs

Understanding the Cultural Shift Toward Crowdfunding

In the early days of crowdfunding, the concept was simple: raise money for a creative project. Whether it was funding an indie film, creating a new gadget, or backing a nonprofit cause, crowdfunding platforms like Kickstarter, Indiegogo, and GoFundMe were born out of the idea that the internet could connect people with shared passions, enabling the collective funding of creative endeavors. But what started as a modest way for creators to seek financial backing has evolved into something far grander. Crowdfunding is now a **cultural revolution**, altering the way we approach entrepreneurship, creativity, and community.

Crowdfunding has gone from a niche experiment to a global phenomenon. In the last decade, the crowdfunding industry has grown exponentially, raising billions of dollars worldwide. It's not just about money—it's about building communities, empowering creators, and rethinking what it means to be an entrepreneur. Platforms that once were primarily used to fund "big ideas" are now giving rise to individual creators, artists, and small businesses with big dreams. Through crowdfunding, creators don't just seek backers—they seek partners. Crowdfunding enables creators to bring their visions to life without needing a traditional publisher, investor, or major brand deal. They can now tap into a **global audience**, get real-time feedback, and iterate on their ideas long before they hit the mass market.

This shift represents a deep cultural change: crowdfunding is now about **community-driven innovation**, and **collective empowerment**. Where once we had gatekeepers in the form of venture capitalists, traditional publishers, and record labels, we now have open-source funding opportunities that allow creators to bypass these barriers. What was once a field exclusive to a few has now become an open market for anyone with an idea and the drive to make it happen.

This democratization of creativity has upended the traditional paradigms of success. As of 2023, over 200,000 projects have been successfully funded on Kickstarter alone, and hundreds of millions of dollars have been raised across dozens of platforms. Crowdfunding has shown us that the power of the collective is far greater than the power of any individual or institution. It has redefined what success looks like—not through financial success alone, but through the ability to create, innovate, and forge lasting relationships with people who share your vision.

In this chapter, we'll explore not just the mechanics of crowdfunding, but how it has become an **essential tool for creators** of all kinds—artists, entrepreneurs, filmmakers, writers, and anyone who seeks to fund a meaningful project. We will also look at how crowdfunding is increasingly being used as a way to **test ideas**, **build brand loyalty**, and **create long-term business models**, rather than just a short-term funding mechanism.

The New Creator Economy

At the heart of this crowdfunding revolution lies the **new creator economy**—an ecosystem where anyone with talent, an idea, and the will to bring it to life can find a path to success. Creators are no longer limited to traditional job markets or financial systems. The rise of social media, content platforms, and crowdfunding sites has allowed a new wave of individuals to transform their hobbies, passions, and side projects into full-time careers. These creators—whether they are YouTubers, podcasters, or independent designers—are using crowdfunding not just to launch individual projects, but to build a business model that is based on **ongoing community support**.

The new creator economy is about **independence**. Crowdfunding allows creators to take ownership of their projects from start to finish—whether they're raising capital, marketing their work, or engaging with their audience. This autonomy is both liberating and empowering, as it enables creators to build their own paths to success without relying on traditional corporate structures.

For many creators, crowdfunding is the first step in a broader entrepreneurial journey. For others, it provides a lifeline to take their passion projects from idea to reality. Platforms like **Patreon**, for example, have allowed creators to cultivate long-term relationships with their audience, turning a one-time fundraising project into a **subscription-based model** that ensures steady, predictable income.

In this creator economy, the line between **creator** and **entrepreneur** is increasingly blurred. Creators today are as much marketers, community managers, and business owners as they are artists or innovators. Crowdfunding has become an integral part of this process. Rather than relying on the whims of investors or publishers, creators are now building businesses around their art, engaging with their communities, and leveraging platforms to raise funds, validate their ideas, and grow their brands.

What makes this ecosystem so unique is the fluidity between **creator** and **audience**. In traditional business models, the audience's role is passive—they consume the product but rarely have a direct role in shaping its creation. In crowdfunding, the audience is an active participant in the process. They're not just backers; they are often **early adopters**, **evangelists**, and **co-creators**.

Crowdfunding platforms have capitalized on this shift, turning **audience engagement** into a central aspect of the funding process. By supporting a creator, backers are often given access to behind-the-scenes content, updates, and even the opportunity to offer feedback on prototypes or ideas. They become emotionally invested in the success of the project, and this emotional connection builds **loyalty**. This relationship is a major departure from traditional models of business, where the consumer is merely a customer.

The Psychological Power of Crowdfunding

One of the key elements that sets crowdfunding apart from traditional fundraising is the **psychological** aspect. Crowdfunding isn't just about asking for money; it's about tapping into the deeper motivations and desires of backers. It's about telling a story that resonates with people on an emotional level, and creating a sense of shared purpose between the creator and their community.

At its core, crowdfunding leverages **social proof**, **scarcity**, **reciprocity**, and **authenticity**—four powerful psychological principles that drive human behavior.

Social proof: When people see that others are supporting a project, they are more likely to support it themselves. Crowdfunding platforms are social spaces where backers can see how many people have already pledged support. This **bandwagon effect** creates momentum, making the project seem more trustworthy and legitimate. Successful crowdfunding campaigns often attract more backers because people want to be a part of something that others are already supporting. It's the modern equivalent of "if everyone else is doing it, it must be worth doing."

Scarcity: Crowdfunding campaigns often include limited-time offers, early bird specials, or exclusive perks. The principle of scarcity plays on our fear of missing out (FOMO), motivating potential backers to act quickly. This is why crowdfunding campaigns often achieve early success in their first 24 to 48 hours—the limited availability of rewards encourages people to take action before they miss their chance.

Reciprocity: This principle is simple: when someone does something for us, we feel compelled to reciprocate. When a creator offers exclusive content, early access to products, or special rewards for their backers, they trigger this powerful sense of indebtedness. Backers are more likely to support a campaign because they feel they are **contributing to something bigger**, and they want to be a part of the creator's success.

Authenticity: One of the most critical elements in successful crowdfunding is the **authenticity** of the creator. Backers are more likely to support campaigns when they feel connected to the creator's story, vision, and mission. Authenticity fosters trust, and in turn, trust builds loyalty. In today's world of digital marketing and influencer culture, the most successful crowdfunding campaigns are those where the creator is transparent, open, and genuine.

Crowdfunding allows creators to **humanize their brand** and establish an emotional connection with their audience in a way that traditional advertising simply cannot. Backers are not just funding a project—they are buying into the creator's story, ethos, and vision. This deep emotional engagement creates a lasting bond that goes far beyond the transactional nature of traditional consumer purchases.

A Global Movement: Crowdfunding as a Cultural Force

Today, crowdfunding is not just a tool for creators—it's a **cultural force** that has fundamentally changed the way we think about entrepreneurship. It's reshaping industries, redefining what it means to be an entrepreneur, and democratizing access to capital in ways that were previously unimaginable.

From **tech startups** to **social causes**, crowdfunding is enabling people to pursue their dreams regardless of their background, geographic location, or financial means. As we enter a more **globalized economy**, crowdfunding platforms allow creators from anywhere in the world to tap into a **global audience**, raising funds and support for their projects across borders. Whether someone is in Berlin or Bangladesh, they can find backers who believe in their vision and are willing to help fund it.

What's particularly exciting is that crowdfunding is not confined to a specific industry or region. Creators from every walk of life—from filmmakers and authors to game designers, health innovators, and even **activists**—are using crowdfunding to bring about **change**. Crowdfunding is giving voice to those who have historically been marginalized or excluded from traditional forms of capital-raising.

Moreover, crowdfunding is contributing to a new **ethos**—one that emphasizes **purpose-driven entrepreneurship** over profit-driven motives. Crowdfunding is often seen as an expression of values; many campaigns now emphasize sustainability, social impact, and community-building. As consumers become more conscious of the ethical dimensions of their spending, crowdfunding allows them to align their financial support with their personal values.

Chapter 2: The Creator's Mindset: Designing a Project to Sell Itself

The Psychological Foundations of a Creator's Mindset

At the core of every successful crowdfunding campaign lies a deep understanding of the creator's mindset. Before you can launch your project and expect others to fund it, you must first **believe in it yourself**. The psychological journey of a creator begins with **confidence**—a belief that your idea is not only valuable but also worthy of attention. Yet, confidence alone isn't enough. There is a crucial step that most creators overlook: aligning their internal motivations with the external realities of crowdfunding success. Cultivating a mindset that integrates passion with practicality, creativity with strategic thinking, is the true foundation of success.

To be successful at crowdfunding, you must first cultivate a sense of purpose. **Purpose-driven creators** are those who understand why they're creating and who they are creating for. This clarity of vision will influence not just the initial pitch, but every interaction with potential backers. When you are deeply rooted in the mission of your project, it becomes easier to express your message clearly and persuasively.

This isn't just about **self-assurance**; it's about having a strong internal compass to navigate the emotional roller coaster that is crowdfunding. When the pressure of deadlines mounts, when the backers aren't coming in as fast as you expected, or when the inevitable setbacks occur, it's your sense of purpose that will carry you through. The most successful creators are those who, above all, have a clear understanding of their "why"—a purpose that resonates not only with themselves but also with their potential supporters. **You must create with a deeper intent, one that serves a larger vision**, whether it's bringing your passion project to life, helping others, or creating change.

A **mindset of resilience** is essential. Launching a crowdfunding campaign is a test of grit and endurance. The process is not just about raising money—it's about maintaining momentum, rallying your community, and learning from setbacks. It's about growing as a creator while you're building your project. Crowdfunding will bring you into direct contact with both the excitement and the challenges of building a business or a brand, and you will encounter plenty of obstacles along the way. **A creator's mindset is one that expects challenges but meets them with optimism, persistence, and a willingness to learn.**

From Passion to Profit: Creating a Project with Marketability

While passion is undoubtedly a critical component of any crowdfunding campaign, passion alone isn't enough. Creators must bridge the gap between their **vision** and the market's **needs**. This is where the concept of **marketability** comes into play. Marketability refers to the extent to which your project resonates with a wide audience, not just in terms of emotional appeal, but also in its ability to meet the desires or solve the problems of potential backers.

The key is to understand that **crowdfunding is as much about sales as it is about creativity**. Even the most creative and innovative projects need to be presented in a way that demonstrates value. It's important to remember that your backers are not just investing in an idea—they're investing in you as a creator, and in the promise that you will deliver on your vision. They are purchasing **an experience**—one that resonates with their needs, desires, or personal values.

To create a project that has inherent marketability, it must be framed within a clear and compelling **value proposition**. This is where your **target audience** comes into play. Who are you speaking to? What do they care about? What problems are they facing that your project can solve? A crowdfunding campaign that is designed without clear attention to these questions is one that will struggle.

Crowdfunding works best when there is a **direct connection** between the creator and their audience. The audience must feel that their support is not just helping the creator, but that they're part of something larger—a shared experience, a movement, or a community. When your project is deeply aligned with what your backers care about, it naturally becomes more marketable. This doesn't mean watering down your vision or chasing trends for the sake of popularity; rather, it's about identifying the intersection between your passion and what resonates with the people you want to reach.

Creating a marketable project means refining your idea to meet the market where it's at. It's about **listening to feedback** and being adaptable enough to pivot when necessary. Successful creators are those who are able to balance **authenticity with appeal**—they stay true to their vision while adapting it in ways that connect with the people who will support them.

Designing Your Project's Value Proposition

The value proposition is the core of your project. It's the promise that you're making to your backers: **"Here's why this project matters, and here's why you should care."** Every successful crowdfunding campaign is built

19

around a clear, compelling value proposition that speaks directly to the needs, emotions, and aspirations of potential backers.

To design a value proposition that will resonate, you need to answer several critical questions:

What is the core problem or need your project solves? Backers don't just fund ideas—they fund solutions. They back creators because they believe in the project's ability to solve a problem, meet a need, or improve their lives in some way. Whether your project is creating a product, offering a service, or supporting a cause, it must clearly demonstrate how it addresses a specific problem or fulfills a need.

What makes your project unique or different from anything else on the market? In a crowded crowdfunding space, differentiation is key. If your project is just like everyone else's, why should someone choose to back you? What makes your offering stand out? It could be the innovative nature of your product, your unique creative process, or even the **personal story** behind your project. By understanding what sets you apart, you can clearly communicate your uniqueness to potential backers.

What is the emotional appeal of your project? Crowdfunding is not just a transactional relationship—it's an emotional one. Backers are drawn to projects that resonate with them on a personal level.

This could be because they believe in your mission, they're passionate about the cause, or they feel a deep connection to the story you're telling. **Emotional connection** is one of the driving factors that motivates people to support a campaign, even when they may not need the product or service being offered. This is why successful crowdfunding campaigns often include **personal stories, human interest angles**, and **authentic, relatable narratives**.

Why should backers act now, and what's in it for them? The urgency to support your campaign must be clear. Why should backers support you now instead of waiting? Is there a limited-time reward, an exclusive opportunity, or early access to something special? Understanding the psychology of scarcity, and using it effectively, will help increase the likelihood of immediate support.

Crafting a value proposition is an iterative process. It starts with the heart of your idea, but as you build your campaign, you will refine it based on feedback and market research. The more you understand what your backers want, the better you can tailor your messaging to resonate with them.

Building Confidence in Your Project

The final aspect of a creator's mindset is the **confidence to take the plunge**. While passion and marketability are essential, none of these will matter if the creator lacks the confidence to follow through on their vision. Confidence comes from two places: **belief in the project itself** and **faith in your ability to execute**.

Before launching a crowdfunding campaign, ask yourself: Do I believe in this project? Do I believe that my backers will benefit from this project in a meaningful way? If your answer to either of these questions is uncertain, then it's time to step back and reassess. Confidence in your idea is not only critical to your mental preparation—it's also contagious. Backers can sense uncertainty, and they are less likely to support a creator who doesn't seem fully committed to their own vision.

Building this confidence often requires **personal growth**. You will have to step outside your comfort zone and embrace a new identity as a **creator-entrepreneur**. This shift isn't just about creating a product or a service—it's about developing the mental fortitude to navigate the highs and lows of a crowdfunding campaign. The more confidence you have in your own ability to succeed, the more confident your backers will feel in supporting you.

Confidence also requires that you develop a mindset of **resilience**. Crowdfunding campaigns are full of ups and downs. You'll face moments when the funding stalls, when you receive negative feedback, or when things don't go according to plan. In these moments, your ability to stay calm, adapt, and keep pushing forward is what separates successful campaigns from those that fail.

To build this type of resilience, it's essential to develop a **growth mindset**—the understanding that challenges are part of the process and that every obstacle is an opportunity to learn and grow. With the right mindset, you will be able to navigate the unpredictable world of crowdfunding with grace and determination, ensuring that your project becomes not just a reality, but a resounding success.

This chapter establishes the foundation for your crowdfunding journey by focusing on the psychological aspects of the creator's mindset. **Confidence, purpose, and resilience** are the internal tools that will drive your success, but they must be paired with strategic thinking and a well-crafted value proposition to ensure your project resonates with the right audience. The combination of these elements—**passion, authenticity, marketability, and emotional connection**—forms the bedrock upon which every successful crowdfunding campaign is built.

Chapter 3: Crowdfunding Platforms: Choosing the Right One for Your Project

The Landscape of Crowdfunding Platforms

The crowdfunding world has evolved significantly since the inception of platforms like Kickstarter and Indiegogo. Today, there are **hundreds of crowdfunding platforms** that cater to different kinds of projects, ranging from technology innovations and social causes to creative arts and community initiatives. As the market grows, it's more important than ever to choose the **right platform** for your specific project. This decision can often make or break a crowdfunding campaign.

But with so many options, how do you decide where to launch your project? The answer lies in understanding both your **project's goals** and the **target audience** you're aiming to reach. Each crowdfunding platform has its own unique culture, user base, features, and fees, and matching your project to the right platform is critical to its success.

The first thing you need to consider is the **type of project** you are launching. Crowdfunding platforms fall into several categories, each with its own strengths and weaknesses. Broadly speaking, the major platforms can be classified into three categories:

General Crowdfunding Platforms – These are the platforms that cater to a wide variety of projects and industries. Examples include **Kickstarter, Indiegogo,** and **GoFundMe.** They are usually the first choice for creators launching tech products, creative projects, or even non-profit causes. These platforms give you access to a broad, global audience, which can be both an advantage and a disadvantage, depending on your project's niche.

Niche Crowdfunding Platforms – These platforms are tailored to specific industries or categories. For example, **Patreon** is focused on subscription-based content creation, and **SeedInvest** specializes in equity crowdfunding for startups. If your project fits into a specific category—like **gaming, fashion,** or **social causes**—niche platforms might give you access to an audience that is more likely to connect with your cause and back your project.

Equity Crowdfunding Platforms – Platforms like **Crowdcube, WeFunder,** and **Republic** enable you to raise capital by offering equity in your business, meaning backers receive a stake in your company. This type of platform is ideal for entrepreneurs looking to scale their business with larger amounts of investment. However, this model requires a solid business plan, compliance with securities laws, and an understanding of the responsibilities involved in sharing ownership of your company.

Key Considerations When Choosing a Crowdfunding Platform

Choosing the right platform for your campaign is about much more than just where you can raise the most funds—it's about selecting a platform that aligns with your **project's goals**, **audience**, and **resources**. Here are the most important factors to consider when making this decision:

Project Type and Platform Fit

The first step is to **identify your project type** and determine which platform is best suited to your goals. Are you launching a product? Are you raising funds for a charitable cause? Do you want to build an audience for your creative work or seek investment for a startup? Each platform has its own strengths, and choosing the one that best matches your project is key.

Kickstarter is best for creative projects that have a strong visual or emotional component, such as films, video games, and new tech products. It has a massive global audience and a proven track record of successfully funding creative ventures.

Indiegogo is great for tech innovations and projects that may require more flexibility in terms of funding models. Indiegogo offers both **flexible funding** (where you keep the money even if you don't meet your goal) and **fixed funding** (where you only keep the money if you meet your goal).

GoFundMe is ideal for personal projects, charitable causes, and community-focused initiatives. Unlike Kickstarter and Indiegogo, GoFundMe is generally **not** reward-based—it's often used for social causes, medical expenses, and personal fundraising.

Patreon is the platform for content creators, such as YouTubers, podcasters, and artists who are looking to build a **subscription-based business model**. It works best for creators who already have an audience and wish to generate ongoing, sustainable income.

SeedInvest, **Crowdcube**, and **Republic** are focused on equity crowdfunding, making them a good choice for entrepreneurs looking to raise capital for startups and scale-ups. This model is more suited for companies seeking larger sums of money from investors in exchange for equity.

Platform Fees and Funding Models

Crowdfunding platforms typically charge a **fee** for using their service, which can vary greatly depending on the platform and the funding model. Most platforms charge a **percentage of the funds raised** (typically 5-10%), plus payment processing fees (usually 3-5%).

However, the platform's fee structure can differ:

Kickstarter and Indiegogo both follow a **"all-or-nothing"** funding model. If you don't reach your funding goal, you don't get any of the funds raised. This creates a sense of urgency and can drive higher levels of engagement, but it also means you risk **not raising any funds** if your campaign falls short of its target.

GoFundMe allows creators to keep the funds raised, even if they don't meet their goal. While this can be advantageous for those with modest goals, it can also make the platform less motivating for backers, who may feel that their money won't go as far without the momentum of meeting a funding target.

Patreon has a unique **subscription-based model**, where creators earn recurring revenue rather than relying on a single fundraising push. Patreon takes a percentage of the monthly payments received, which is typically **5-12%** depending on the creator's tier.

Equity crowdfunding platforms like **SeedInvest** and **WeFunder** charge fees that are typically higher, as they involve more regulatory oversight and are designed for larger-scale investment opportunities.

In addition to platform fees, be sure to research the **funding models** available. Some platforms offer **fixed funding**, where you must hit your goal to receive any funds, while others offer **flexible funding**, allowing you to keep whatever you raise. The choice of funding model should reflect your financial goals, the risk tolerance of your project, and how confident you are in reaching your goal.

Audience Reach and Demographics

The **audience** of a crowdfunding platform is perhaps one of the most important considerations. Different platforms attract different types of backers, and choosing the right one can give you access to a specific demographic that aligns with your project. Here's a closer look at the audiences you'll find on popular platforms:

Kickstarter tends to attract backers who are passionate about supporting **creative, innovative** projects. It is highly competitive, with a large number of projects vying for attention, but also offers a substantial pool of backers who are experienced in crowdfunding.

Indiegogo has a diverse audience that spans both **early adopters** and individuals who are looking for **unique gadgets** or **technology innovations**. It's ideal for creators who have products that appeal to a tech-savvy crowd.

GoFundMe attracts a more **personal** audience, as it's often used for medical expenses, emergency relief, and community-based causes. This platform's backers are typically driven by **empathy and social connection** rather than the desire for exclusive rewards.

Patreon works best for creators with an existing audience—whether it's YouTubers, podcasters, or musicians. Patreon's audience is engaged in **ongoing support**, so it's less about one-time funding and more about cultivating long-term relationships with backers.

Equity crowdfunding platforms such as **Crowdcube** or **Republic** attract a different kind of backer—**investors** looking to take an equity stake in a growing business. These platforms are better suited to startups that are seeking significant financial backing and are willing to give away a portion of ownership in exchange for funding.

To evaluate the audience of a platform, check out the projects that have successfully raised funds in your category. You can also look at the types of rewards being offered, the types of backers leaving comments, and the kinds of social media engagement campaigns are generating. A platform's **audience fit** with your project is often more important than the size of the platform itself. The most successful campaigns are often those that align well with the platform's user base, even if that audience is smaller.

Support, Resources, and Community

Not all crowdfunding platforms are created equal when it comes to the level of support and resources they provide to creators. Some platforms offer **dedicated campaign managers**, **marketing resources**, and **community-building tools** to help you succeed. Others may simply provide the platform and leave it to you to figure everything out.

Kickstarter has a large community of creators and backers, and it offers resources such as success stories, FAQs, and a blog filled with tips. Kickstarter's **Creator Handbook** is a comprehensive guide to running a successful campaign. While it doesn't offer personal campaign management, its community is active, and there are many tools for collaboration.

Indiegogo offers a **"Launchpad"** service to help you with campaign management, providing advice on marketing, design, and even **product fulfillment**. Indiegogo also offers a suite of **campaign optimization tools** to help you track your progress and improve your strategy.

Patreon, as a subscription-based platform, emphasizes **creator support** and offers a variety of resources,

Chapter 4: Crafting a Winning Campaign Page

The First Impression: Your Campaign Page as a Sales Tool

When launching a crowdfunding campaign, your **campaign page** is often the first thing potential backers will see, and it needs to capture their attention quickly. Just like any sales tool, your campaign page must engage, inform, and persuade. In a sea of competing projects, a **well-crafted page** stands out, helping you build trust, convey your passion, and ultimately secure the funds you need.

Think of your campaign page as a **storytelling platform**. It should clearly communicate what your project is about, why it matters, and what makes it unique. The goal is to turn your backers into partners who feel emotionally connected to your mission and see value in supporting it. This means your page needs to be **visually appealing, easy to navigate**, and **compelling** in both its text and its multimedia content.

There are several key components to creating a campaign page that converts casual visitors into committed backers.

Key Elements of a High-Converting Campaign Page

Compelling Project Title and Tagline

The first thing people will notice when they visit your page is your **project title**. This title should be short, memorable, and clearly describe your project. Follow this up with a **catchy tagline** or slogan that explains your project's value proposition in one or two lines. Make sure these first elements grab attention and spark curiosity—this is your elevator pitch in written form.

For example, if you're crowdfunding a new app, the title could be something like "HealthMate: The Smart Fitness App That Gets You Results" and the tagline could elaborate: "Join the future of fitness with real-time AI coaching to help you reach your goals faster."

Engaging Project Video

One of the most important elements of your campaign page is the **video**. Studies show that campaigns with videos raise **50% more money** than those without. This is because video allows you to connect with potential backers on an emotional level, show them your passion, and bring your project to life.

Your video should be **concise, professional,** and **authentic**. It doesn't need to be Hollywood-level production quality, but it must communicate clearly what your project is, why you're passionate about it, and how it will benefit backers. Include a personal introduction, demonstrate your product (if applicable), and share why you're the right person to bring this vision to life.

Clear Project Description

After the video, your project description is your next most important tool for conversion. This section should provide a clear, **detailed explanation** of your project. Explain:

What your project is.
Why it matters (the problem it solves or the value it adds).
How it will work (for products, show the prototype or sketches).
Who you are and why you're the best person/team to deliver this.

Your project description should answer the **who, what, why, and how** in a way that's engaging and easy to follow. Break up the text into short paragraphs and use headings, bullet points, and visuals to make the page more digestible. Don't overwhelm visitors with too much information, but make sure you cover the key aspects that potential backers need to know.

Reward Tiers

One of the core elements of crowdfunding is the rewards structure. Offering **tiers of rewards** that appeal to different levels of support can increase your chances of success.

Start with **low-cost rewards** for backers who just want to show their support, such as a thank-you note or digital content (e.g., wallpapers or updates).
Provide **mid-level rewards** like early access to your product, limited edition items, or special recognition.
Premium rewards should appeal to your most dedicated supporters. These might include a high-end version of your product, a personalized experience, or a VIP experience.

Make sure the rewards are well-thought-out and **value-driven**—they should reflect the **backers' investment** while making them feel appreciated. **Transparency** is key here, so clarify exactly what backers will receive and when they can expect it. Clear timelines are essential for managing expectations and building trust.

Visual Design and Branding

Your campaign page needs to be **visually compelling**. Use high-quality images, consistent branding, and a clean layout that supports the message you want to convey. The design should feel **professional**, but also reflect the **personality** of your project. Your visuals can include:

Product images: Show your product in different angles and settings. If it's still in development, consider using mockups or renders.
Behind-the-scenes shots: Show your team at work or give insight into the creative process.
Infographics: Use simple visuals to explain how your product works or highlight key benefits.
Branding elements: Use colors, fonts, and logos that reflect the tone and spirit of your project.

A well-designed campaign page looks polished but doesn't distract from the message. Keep the **focus** on your project's core value.

Social Proof and Testimonials

Trust is everything when it comes to crowdfunding. **Social proof**—such as testimonials, media coverage, or endorsements from respected figures—can play a pivotal role in convincing potential backers that your project is credible and worth supporting.

If you have **early supporters**, showcase their testimonials or any relevant press you've received. You can also include **reviews or quotes** from influencers, beta testers, or people who've seen your product in action. Positive feedback from others will help validate your project and give new backers confidence in their decision to support you.

A Sense of Urgency

Crowdfunding is often successful when it taps into the **urgency** of limited-time offers. You can create a sense of urgency through **time-limited rewards**, **early bird offers**, or by highlighting how much funding is left to reach your goal. Phrases like "**only 50 early bird spots available**" or "**48 hours left to support**" can nudge people to act quickly.

Urgency doesn't just have to be about deadlines; it can also involve highlighting the **impact** of their support. Remind your backers how their contribution will make a difference and how their early support will help bring the project to life.

Final Touches: Refining Your Page for Maximum Impact

Once you have all the essential components in place, the final step is to **refine your campaign page** for maximum impact. Here are a few extra touches to consider:

Proofread: Spelling and grammatical errors can hurt your credibility, so ensure your copy is polished.
Test your layout: Make sure everything is mobile-friendly, as a large percentage of backers browse campaigns on their phones.
Link to social media: Make it easy for backers to share your project by including social media buttons, shareable links, and clear calls to action.

A compelling, well-organized campaign page can dramatically improve your chances of success. It's your **virtual storefront**—treat it like one. Make sure it reflects your vision, tells your story authentically, and presents your rewards in an irresistible way.

A great campaign page is more than just a place to showcase your idea—it's your main sales tool. By making it visually appealing, clear, and emotionally compelling, you create an experience that will **engage** backers and motivate them to support your vision. A well-designed page can set the stage for the ultimate success of your campaign, helping you meet your funding goals and beyond.

Chapter 5: Building and Engaging Your Community Before You Launch

The Power of Community in Crowdfunding

Before you even think about launching your crowdfunding campaign, it's crucial to understand the **importance of community**. A crowdfunding campaign is not just about raising money; it's about creating a movement. Crowdfunding is inherently **social**, and your ability to **build and nurture a community** around your project will have a direct impact on the success of your campaign.

A strong, engaged community will not only support you financially—they'll also **spread the word**, **offer feedback, serve as ambassadors**, and help create buzz long before your campaign goes live. The most successful crowdfunding campaigns are not built on one-time transactions; they thrive because they have an engaged base of **loyal supporters** who are personally invested in your success. They don't just fund your project; they help you shape it, elevate it, and ensure its success.

In this chapter, we'll explore **strategies for building your community**, how to **engage with your audience**, and why this process **should begin long before your campaign launch**.

Why Start Building a Community Before You Launch?

It may seem tempting to launch your campaign and immediately start pushing for funds, but starting the community-building process **well in advance** is a crucial step that can't be overlooked. Here are some of the reasons why:

Early Backers as Catalysts: The first 30% of your funding typically comes from your **immediate network**—friends, family, and people who know you or are familiar with your brand. Building a community before you launch means you already have a pool of **early supporters** who can contribute to your campaign when it goes live, giving you the momentum you need to attract larger backers.

Trust and Credibility: Crowdfunding relies heavily on **trust**. People are more likely to back a project if they feel they are part of an engaged community. By nurturing a community before you launch, you help establish **credibility** and **authenticity**, which builds trust with potential backers.

Word-of-Mouth Marketing: Community members who feel connected to your project will naturally become your **brand advocates**. They'll spread the word to their social networks, recommend your campaign to others, and drive traffic to your page. By building a loyal community, you get **organic promotion** without the hefty costs of paid advertising.

Feedback and Refinement: Your community isn't just a group of people to ask for funds—it's also a **valuable source of feedback**. Engaging with your audience before launch allows you to test ideas, get opinions on your rewards, and understand how your project resonates with people. By taking their feedback into account, you can refine your campaign and product to make it even better.

Strategies for Building Your Community

Building a community for your crowdfunding campaign requires **consistent effort, engagement,** and **authenticity**. Here are several key strategies for developing a strong, supportive group of backers before you launch your campaign:

Create a Strong Brand Identity

Your community needs to know **who you are, what you stand for,** and **what your project represents**. Your project's **brand identity** is what will draw people in and connect them to your mission.

Develop a clear message: What's your project's purpose? Why should people care about it? Define your vision, mission, and values so your community knows exactly what they're supporting.

Create a compelling narrative: Your backers will want to know **why you're doing this**. Sharing your **personal story**, why you created the project, and your motivations will help people connect with you on a deeper level.

Visual identity: Consistent **visual branding** (colors, logo, font) should be reflected across your campaign page, social media profiles, and any promotional material you create. This helps to reinforce your identity and makes your project instantly recognizable.

Build an Email List

One of the most effective ways to build a community before your crowdfunding campaign goes live is by creating an **email list**. Email is a direct line of communication with your most engaged supporters, and it's a critical tool for driving your campaign's launch.

Here's how you can grow your email list:

Create a lead magnet: Offer something of value to potential supporters in exchange for their email addresses. This could be an **exclusive preview**, **early access** to your product, or a **special resource** that ties into your project. Make sure it's something your target audience would find valuable.

Landing page: Build a simple landing page where people can sign up for your email list. This page should explain the project and include an option to **receive updates**. A strong **call to action** (CTA) is essential to prompt visitors to join your email list.

Offer incentives: Once you have an email list, you can nurture it by offering early bird pricing, exclusive content, or behind-the-scenes looks at your project. The more value you provide, the more likely your subscribers are to **convert into backers**.

Leverage Social Media

Social media is one of the most powerful tools for building a community, as it allows you to reach a wide audience and engage with potential backers in real time. But **social media engagement** is about more than just promoting your campaign—it's about **creating conversations**, **sharing stories**, and **building relationships**.

Start early: Don't wait until your campaign is live to start posting. Begin sharing content that's relevant to your project **months in advance**. Create teasers, polls, or countdowns to generate excitement.

Consistent content: Post regularly to keep your audience engaged. Share updates about your project's progress, introduce team members, or give sneak peeks into your creative process. Use **Instagram stories**, **Twitter threads**, and **Facebook groups** to keep your community in the loop.

Interact with your audience: Social media is a **two-way street**. Respond to comments, answer questions, and thank your followers for their support. Engaging with your community will make them feel valued and increase their likelihood of backing your campaign.

Collaborations and partnerships: Partner with influencers, industry experts, or other creators who align with your project. Having others promote your project to their followers can greatly expand your reach.

Utilize Online Communities and Forums

There are thousands of online forums and communities where potential backers are already gathered. Joining these platforms and participating in conversations can be a great way to build interest in your project before launch.

Reddit: Subreddits like r/crowdfunding, r/startups, and others related to your project's industry are excellent places to engage with people who might be interested in supporting your campaign. Just be sure to **follow the community guidelines** and avoid overtly promotional posts.

Facebook Groups: Join relevant Facebook groups where your target audience hangs out. Engage in discussions, ask questions, and share your expertise. Once you've established a relationship with the group, you can start talking about your project in a more natural way.

Discord and Slack: If your project targets a **tech-savvy** or **niche** audience, platforms like Discord or Slack can be ideal places to build a dedicated community. Set up channels for backers to discuss your project, offer feedback, and stay updated.

Email groups and newsletters: Find newsletters in your niche or industry that feature new crowdfunding projects. Pitch your campaign to these newsletters, or reach out to communities that focus on crowdfunding to help you build an early audience.

Host Pre-Launch Events

To create anticipation for your campaign, consider hosting **pre-launch events** that allow potential backers to interact with you and learn more about your project. These events can take many forms, such as:

Webinars: Host a live Q&A session where you discuss your project and answer questions from your audience. This will help establish your credibility and build excitement.

Product demos: If your campaign involves a physical product, consider hosting a **live demonstration** on Facebook Live, Instagram Live, or Zoom to give potential backers a closer look at your creation.

Meetups or live chats: If feasible, meet potential backers in person or through virtual meetups. Offering a chance to **connect with you directly** builds trust and humanizes your campaign.

Provide Early Access to Backers

People love to feel like they are part of an **exclusive group**. Consider offering **early access** to backers who are interested in being part of the campaign before it officially launches. This could involve offering:

Exclusive behind-the-scenes content
Pre-launch discounts or **early bird pricing**
First access to your product or service

These types of perks make your backers feel special and valued, helping to build a sense of community and anticipation.

Maintaining Momentum Throughout the Campaign

Building a community doesn't stop once you launch your crowdfunding campaign. It's essential to continue **engaging your community** throughout the entire campaign, keeping them updated on your progress and showing them how their support is making a difference. Regular updates, behind-the-scenes looks, and ongoing interactions will help keep your community invested in the success of your project.

By creating a **strong, engaged community** before your campaign launches, you set yourself up for **long-term success**. A loyal, motivated group of backers can be your most powerful asset, helping you reach your funding goal and making your project a reality.

Chapter 6: Setting Realistic Goals and Expectations for Your Campaign

The Foundation of Your Success: Defining Your Goals

In crowdfunding, setting the right goals is one of the most critical steps in ensuring the success of your campaign. But goal-setting isn't just about choosing an arbitrary number you hope to raise. It's about being **strategic**, **realistic**, and aligning your funding targets with the needs of your project and the expectations of your backers.

Your **goal** serves as a guidepost for your entire campaign. It tells potential backers how much you need to bring your idea to life, and it helps you define what success looks like. However, it's essential to approach this with a combination of ambition and practicality. Setting a goal that is too high could discourage backers, while setting a goal that is too low may leave you short of the resources needed to complete your project. A well-thought-out goal should **inspire trust**, **create urgency**, and **motivate action**.

In this chapter, we'll delve into **how to set your crowdfunding goal**, what factors influence it, and how to manage your expectations throughout the campaign.

Key Considerations When Setting Your Funding Goal

Understand Your Project's True Cost

The first step in setting a realistic crowdfunding goal is to have a thorough understanding of what it will cost to bring your project to life. This includes more than just the cost of **production**—you need to account for **marketing, shipping, fees, rewards fulfillment**, and any other **hidden expenses**.

Production costs: These are the costs associated with creating your product or service. If you're crowdfunding a physical product, this might include the cost of raw materials, manufacturing, packaging, and quality control. **Marketing and promotion**: While crowdfunding is inherently a form of marketing, you may still need to spend money to promote your campaign, whether through social media ads, influencer partnerships, or hiring a PR agency to help get the word out. **Reward fulfillment**: The rewards you offer to backers will also come with a cost. Shipping fees, packaging, and the time involved in assembling and distributing these rewards should be accounted for.

Crowdfunding platform fees: Don't forget that crowdfunding platforms, such as Kickstarter or Indiegogo, take a percentage of the funds you raise. This is usually around **5%** but can be higher depending on the platform and payment processors.

Unexpected costs: Always factor in a buffer for unexpected expenses. Manufacturing delays, price hikes, or unforeseen challenges may arise, so it's a good idea to have an extra **10-20%** built into your funding goal.

By doing a detailed budget breakdown, you can ensure that your goal reflects the true cost of your project and that you won't end up scrambling to cover additional expenses once the campaign is underway.

Evaluate Your Backer Potential

When setting your goal, it's crucial to have a clear sense of your **target audience** and how many people are likely to support your project. This is where your **community-building efforts** (which we discussed in the previous chapter) will pay off. If you've built a solid following on social media, through email lists, or by engaging in online communities, you'll have a better idea of the number of **potential backers** who are interested in your project.

Use this information to calculate how many people you will need to support your goal at varying levels. You can use a simple formula like this to get started:

Total goal amount / Average backer contribution = Number of backers needed

For example, if your goal is $10,000 and the average backer pledges $50, you'll need **200 backers** to reach your target. Of course, you might have **higher reward tiers** with bigger contributions, but this gives you a rough idea of the audience size you need to engage to meet your goal.

Understanding the number of people required to back your project will also give you insight into your **marketing strategy**. Are you targeting a **niche group** of 100 highly engaged supporters? Or do you plan on reaching a **larger audience** who may only donate small amounts? Your goal should align with the audience you're able to connect with.

Consider the Platform's Success Rate

Different crowdfunding platforms have different success rates, and these rates are affected by the project category, the quality of the campaign, and the amount of work put into **community engagement** and **marketing**. Before setting your goal, research the typical funding goals for projects in your category on your chosen platform. For example:

Kickstarter has an average success rate of around **37%** for projects that reach their funding goal, but the rate can vary dramatically by industry. Technology and design projects tend to have higher success rates, while some categories (like arts and crafts) may have more modest outcomes.
Indiegogo often sees a higher percentage of **flexible funding** (where you can keep whatever funds you raise, even if you don't hit your goal), but success rates may be lower than Kickstarter's.

Looking at your chosen platform's data can help you determine a **realistic target** for your campaign. Setting a goal that's in line with your platform's **average success rate** can also help to build confidence with backers. A funding goal that seems too high may appear **unachievable** and deter potential supporters from backing your project. On the other hand, a goal that's too low might not provide enough funds to complete the project, which could hurt your credibility.

Create Stretch Goals to Maintain Momentum

Once you've set your initial funding goal, consider creating **stretch goals**—additional milestones that are unlocked when your campaign exceeds its initial goal. Stretch goals are a great way to:

Increase excitement as you approach your target.
Encourage additional contributions from backers who want to see the campaign succeed.
Provide **new rewards** or bonuses to your backers as you unlock new goals.

For example, if you're crowdfunding a new board game and your goal is $10,000, you could set a stretch goal at $15,000 to fund additional artwork or game pieces. You could then create another stretch goal at $20,000 to add new expansion packs or exclusive content.

Stretch goals help to keep your community engaged and excited, especially if they've already pledged and want to see your project succeed beyond the initial goal. **Transparency** about how these stretch goals will be achieved is key to keeping backers motivated and on board.

Plan for the "All-or-Nothing" Model

Crowdfunding platforms like Kickstarter and GoFundMe typically operate on an **all-or-nothing** model, meaning that if you don't reach your goal by the campaign's deadline, you receive no funding. This can create additional pressure to meet your target, but it also provides a built-in **incentive** for backers to contribute sooner rather than later.

If you're using an all-or-nothing platform, it's even more important to ensure your funding goal is **achievable**. While setting an ambitious target is fine, you must have a clear plan to get there. Underestimating your backer potential or setting your goal too high may result in a **failed campaign**, and that can harm your credibility.

For backers, knowing that your goal is all-or-nothing helps them feel more confident about contributing, as they know the project won't proceed unless it reaches its full target. It also means you'll have **all the necessary funds** to carry out your project as promised.

Managing Expectations During Your Campaign

While setting realistic goals is critical, managing your expectations during the campaign is just as important. Crowdfunding campaigns are often filled with **unexpected twists** and **unpredictable momentum**. Here are some tips to help you maintain perspective:

Be prepared for slow periods: Crowdfunding campaigns often start strong and then experience a plateau in the middle. This is a normal part of the process, and it's important not to get discouraged. Use these slower periods to re-engage your community, promote your campaign through targeted ads or influencer partnerships, and adjust your strategy if needed.

Stay transparent: Keep your backers informed about your progress, including any challenges you encounter. If something isn't going according to plan, share it with your community. Transparency builds trust and ensures that your backers are supportive when you need them most.

Set mini-milestones: In addition to your main funding goal, consider setting smaller milestones that you can celebrate along the way. These mini-goals will help maintain momentum and encourage backers to keep pushing your campaign toward its full funding target.

Conclusion

Setting a realistic funding goal is essential to the success of your crowdfunding campaign. It requires a deep understanding of your project's costs, the size of your audience, and the dynamics of the crowdfunding platform. While your goal should reflect the true cost of your project, it should also be achievable, backed by a strong marketing plan, and supported by a loyal community. By planning for success and managing expectations throughout the process, you can ensure that your campaign reaches its potential and meets your funding needs.

In this chapter, we explored the importance of setting a **realistic and achievable crowdfunding goal** and the factors that can influence it. By understanding your costs, evaluating your backer potential, and aligning your goal with platform expectations, you can set yourself up for a successful campaign. Additionally, by creating stretch goals and planning for the all-or-nothing model, you can keep your backers excited and invested in your project. Managing expectations throughout the campaign will help you stay focused and maintain

Chapter 7: Crafting an Irresistible Campaign Page

The Anatomy of a High-Converting Crowdfunding Page

Your crowdfunding campaign page is the **face** of your project—it's where you'll make your pitch, showcase your vision, and ultimately convince people to back your idea. But creating a compelling campaign page isn't just about listing features or showing off a cool product; it's about **telling a story**, building trust, and **emotionally connecting** with potential backers.

A great campaign page does much more than present information—it **persuades, inspires**, and **drives action**. Think of it as your campaign's most powerful sales tool, but with an added layer of **authenticity** and **excitement** that crowdfunding platforms foster. If done right, your page will serve as a visual and emotional anchor that guides backers through your campaign, turning curiosity into commitment.

In this chapter, we'll break down the key elements of a **high-converting crowdfunding page** and how you can structure it for maximum impact.

The Headline: A Powerful First Impression

The headline of your crowdfunding page is your **first opportunity** to grab potential backers' attention. It's the equivalent of a **hook**—it needs to spark curiosity, make a promise, and encapsulate the essence of your project in just a few words. A great headline is **clear, concise**, and **compelling**. It should answer the question: "Why should I care about this project?"

Key tips for writing a great headline:

Make it short and snappy: Ideally, keep your headline to under 10 words. It should be easily scannable and convey the core value of your project.

Focus on the benefit: Rather than focusing on features, highlight the **outcome** or **transformation** that backers will experience by supporting your campaign.

Use action-oriented language: Action verbs like "create," "build," "transform," and "join" invoke a sense of urgency and action. Think about how you want your backers to feel when they read it.

For example:

"Bring the Future of Gaming to Life"
"Help Us Redesign the Backpack for the Modern Traveler"
"Fuel Our Mission to Rebuild Endangered Habitats"

The headline should clearly communicate **what your project is**, **why it matters**, and why it's worth backing.

The Video: Emotionally Engaging and Persuasive

Your campaign video is arguably the **most powerful** element of your crowdfunding page. It's your chance to introduce yourself, your team, and your project in a way that is **personal, compelling,** and **emotionally engaging**. A well-crafted video can immediately connect with potential backers and give them the confidence that you're a **credible** creator who is **passionate** and committed to delivering on your promises.

What makes a great crowdfunding video?

Start strong: The first few seconds of your video should immediately grab attention. Don't wait for the viewer to "warm up"—lead with your most compelling hook.

Keep it concise: Most crowdfunding videos should be between **1 and 2 minutes** long. Focus on the most critical points—why your project is important, how it will impact backers, and what makes it unique.

Tell a story: Don't just explain what your project is—**tell a story** that explains why it exists. Why did you start this journey? What problem are you solving? Why does it matter to the world? Personal stories and emotional appeal work wonders in building trust.

Show, don't just tell: Use visuals to demonstrate the product or concept, behind-the-scenes footage, testimonials, or examples of your work. People want to **see** what their money will go toward.

Use a call-to-action: At the end of the video, remind viewers of the **next step**. Encourage them to pledge, share the campaign, or get involved in some other way.

A high-quality video doesn't necessarily mean it needs to be overly polished or professional. The key is authenticity—showing backers that you are passionate, committed, and willing to go the extra mile to bring your idea to life. If you can evoke emotion and demonstrate the real-world impact of your project, you will have a far better chance of success.

The Project Description: Clear, Concise, and Persuasive

While your video is the emotional anchor of your page, the **project description** provides the **details**—the **why**, the **how**, and the **what**. This section should be written in a way that is easy to read, engaging, and answers all the important questions backers might have.

Key elements to include in your project description:

The Problem: Explain the problem your project addresses. Why does it matter? Who is affected? You need to frame the project as a solution to a **real-world problem**.

The Solution: How does your project solve this problem? This is where you talk about your product, service, or idea. Be clear, specific, and avoid jargon—potential backers need to understand exactly what you are offering.

The Benefits: Go beyond the features of your product. What do backers gain from supporting your campaign? Whether it's **personal empowerment**, a **better quality of life**, or **supporting a cause**, make sure the benefits are **clear**.

Your Story: Share your journey and why you're the right person to bring this project to life. Whether it's your **passion**, **experience**, or **commitment**, backers want to know why **you** are the one to bet on.

Timeline: Backers want to know when they can expect their rewards. Give them an honest, achievable timeline that includes milestones for production, fulfillment, and delivery. Avoid promising too much too soon—**realistic timelines** will help build trust.

Risks and Challenges: Be transparent about the challenges you might face. Acknowledging the risks of your project and showing how you plan to overcome them will **increase trust**. Backers understand that every project has risks, but transparency shows that you're **prepared** and **responsible**.

The Rewards: Crafting the Perfect Incentives

Your reward tiers are a critical part of your crowdfunding campaign. They give backers an incentive to contribute to your campaign and serve as a **thank-you** for their support. But rewards should do more than just offer products—they should offer **value**, and they should **align with your backers' motivations**.

Key considerations for creating great rewards:

Offer value at every level: Your rewards should be tiered in a way that makes backers feel like they're **getting a good deal** at every contribution level. The higher the pledge, the better the reward should be—but even your smallest tiers should offer something meaningful.

Exclusive rewards: People love feeling like they're part of something special, so offering **limited edition** items, early access, or behind-the-scenes content is an effective way to entice backers.

Create emotional connection: Consider offering rewards that allow backers to feel like they are part of your story. Personalized messages, credits on your website, or having their name included in your product can make a huge emotional impact.

Ensure fulfillment is realistic: Make sure that your reward structure is feasible and that you can realistically fulfill them. Over-promising can backfire, so focus on rewards that you can deliver with excellence and on time.

Example of tier structure:

$10 – Thank-you shout-out on social media
$25 – Early access to the product and digital content
$50 – Exclusive backer T-shirt and digital thank-you note
$100 – Limited-edition product with personalized note

It's important that your reward levels match the **emotional engagement** you're aiming for and that the rewards are appropriately scaled. Offering **value** without overextending yourself is key.

The Visuals: Bring Your Project to Life

Visuals play a **crucial role** in how potential backers perceive your project. The images and graphics on your campaign page should visually communicate the essence of your project, create excitement, and enhance your storytelling.

Key visuals to include:

High-quality images: Use clear, high-resolution images to showcase your product, prototype, or concept. Show different angles, uses, or applications to give potential backers a full sense of what they're supporting.
Infographics: Visuals like charts, timelines, and diagrams help explain complex ideas or processes in a simple, digestible format.
Behind-the-scenes photos: Sharing photos of your **creative process**, team, or manufacturing gives backers a personal connection to your project.
Mockups or prototypes: If your project is still in development, showing rough mockups or prototypes helps backers understand what to expect. It also demonstrates your progress, showing that the project is **actively moving forward**.

The Call to Action (CTA): Urging Backers to Act

Finally, your crowdfunding page should have a **clear and compelling call to action** that encourages people to take the next step. Whether it's backing the project, sharing it on social media, or signing up for email updates, your CTA should be prominent, easy to find, and directly related to your campaign's goals.

Chapter 8: Building Momentum and Marketing Your Campaign

Why Building Momentum Matters

In crowdfunding, momentum is **everything**. The first 48 hours and the last 48 hours of your campaign are crucial. These are the periods when you can see the most **backer activity**, and they often determine whether or not you succeed in reaching your goal. But building momentum isn't just about throwing together a few social media posts and hoping for the best—it's about carefully creating a **strategy** that generates interest, builds anticipation, and encourages sustained engagement throughout your campaign.

Momentum doesn't just magically appear—it's something you **build** before your campaign even launches and then continue to fuel once your campaign goes live. In this chapter, we'll cover how to **generate excitement**, maintain interest, and keep backers engaged through the **marketing efforts** that will propel your crowdfunding campaign toward success.

Pre-Launch: Setting the Stage for Success

Building momentum starts long before you press "launch" on your crowdfunding campaign. The **pre-launch phase** is essential for preparing your audience, generating buzz, and ensuring that you have a strong base of supporters lined up before the campaign goes live.

Build a Landing Page and Capture Emails

Before your campaign launches, create a **landing page** that describes your project and encourages people to sign up for email updates. Use this landing page to build a list of **interested potential backers**. This will give you a ready-made audience that you can notify when your campaign goes live, and it helps **generate early interest**.

Offer an incentive: Consider offering early backers an incentive to sign up, like exclusive access to limited rewards or special bonuses once the campaign launches. **Drive traffic**: Promote this landing page on your website, through social media, and with any existing email lists or networks you have. The more email sign-ups you gather, the stronger your pre-launch momentum will be.

Engage with Your Audience Early

Begin engaging with potential backers on social media and other channels **early**—ideally several months before your campaign goes live. Share updates about the project's progress, behind-the-scenes content, and sneak peeks. Make sure to engage in conversations and respond to questions to build a community around your project.

Leverage social media: Create profiles or hashtags on Instagram, Twitter, or TikTok that are dedicated to your project. Share regular updates and interact with your followers.

Use storytelling: Share why you're passionate about the project and what inspired you to start it. People connect with stories, and telling yours can build excitement.

Build Relationships with Influencers and Media

In the pre-launch phase, begin identifying influencers or bloggers within your industry who may be interested in your project. Building relationships with these individuals can help generate early **media coverage** and **social proof** for your campaign.

Reach out to influencers and ask if they'd be willing to share your project when it goes live. This could be in the form of a social media post, an article, or even a product review if they're willing to try your product before launch.

Media outreach: Write press releases or pitch your story to journalists who cover crowdfunding, your industry, or product category. Getting coverage before your launch will help you build buzz and ensure you hit the ground running when the campaign starts.

Prepare Your Backer Community

Start growing a community that is **invested** in your project even before you go live. Whether through a **Facebook group**, **Discord channel**, or **email list**, get your supporters involved in the creation process and keep them informed about your campaign timeline.

Early feedback: Ask for feedback on your product or campaign materials. This not only helps you improve but also strengthens the feeling of **ownership** and **participation** among your backers.
Preview rewards: Share sneak peeks of your reward tiers and exclusive early-bird specials. This builds anticipation and excitement.

Launch: Creating Initial Buzz and Early Backers

The first 48 hours of your crowdfunding campaign are critical. This is when you need to generate **early momentum** to get your campaign off the ground. Backers are more likely to back your project early on if they see it already gaining traction.

Push for Early Backers

In the first hours or days of your campaign, focus on getting **early backers**—especially those who have been following your pre-launch efforts. Send out email updates to everyone on your mailing list and let them know your campaign is live. Be sure to share your **campaign link** widely across social media, blogs, and other communication channels.

Incentivize early backers: Offer special **early-bird rewards** for those who back your project within the first 48 hours. This can help **create urgency** and incentivize people to act quickly.

Social proof: As you get early backers, share the news. Announce milestones like "50% funded in the first 12 hours" to build credibility and show that others are already supporting your project.

Leverage Your Network

Reach out to friends, family, colleagues, and industry contacts to give your campaign an initial push. Personal outreach can help you get that critical early support and **build momentum**.

Personalized messages: Send personal messages to those in your network, asking them to back your project or share it with their own networks. The more **personal and heartfelt** the ask, the better.

Activate your community: Encourage your followers on social media to help spread the word. Remind them of your campaign, share updates, and ask them to share with their own network. Word of mouth is **powerful** in crowdfunding.

Use Paid Advertising Strategically

If you have a marketing budget, consider using **paid ads** to increase visibility in the first days. Facebook and Instagram ads, Google ads, or even YouTube video ads can help reach a wider audience and build **momentum** fast.

Focus your ads on specific interests, keywords, or demographics that align with your target backer audience.
Set a **small daily budget** for the first few days of your campaign and adjust based on the results.

Mid-Campaign: Keeping the Momentum Alive

Once the initial excitement starts to fade, the key is to **keep the momentum going** and maintain interest throughout the campaign's life. Crowdfunding campaigns often experience a plateau in the middle, but this doesn't mean your work is done. Use this time to re-engage with your audience and remind them why your project matters.

Maintain Regular Updates

One of the best ways to maintain momentum during the middle of your campaign is through **regular updates**. These updates can be in the form of:

Progress reports: Share how far you've come and how much closer you are to your goal. Keep backers informed on your production, goals, and any new developments.
Behind-the-scenes content: Post photos or videos that showcase your journey, such as production updates, team activities, or new design iterations.
Shout-outs to backers: Celebrate milestones, such as reaching a funding target or getting a press mention. Acknowledge your backers and show appreciation.

Launch a New Stretch Goal

If you've met your initial funding goal, use the opportunity to announce **stretch goals**. These additional goals help keep your backers excited and engaged while motivating others to back your campaign.

Stretch goals can include extra features, bonus rewards, or additional product variants. Keep backers involved by revealing these goals gradually.

Host Live Events

Live events (via Facebook Live, Instagram Live, or Zoom) are a great way to **re-engage your audience**. Host Q&A sessions, do live product demos, or even bring in special guests to talk about your project.

Live events are interactive, which makes them more engaging for backers.
Use these events to show your passion for the project and directly engage with your audience in real time.

Collaborate with Influencers

Continue to work with influencers or press outlets to extend the campaign's reach. **Guest posts**, **interviews**, or **collaborative content** can help bring fresh eyes to your campaign and generate more buzz.

Final Stretch: Creating Urgency and Closing Strong

In the last 48 hours of your campaign, you want to generate a **surge of activity** that can push you over the top. This is where you can capitalize on urgency and excitement to maximize contributions.

Remind Backers of the Deadline

As the deadline approaches, **remind** your backers that time is running out. Use email, social media, and updates to encourage them to act now.

Countdowns: Use countdown timers on your campaign page, social media, and email to visually show how little time is left.
Final call: Send out a final reminder email or social post on the last day, offering a **last-chance opportunity** for backers to get involved.

Offer Final Promotions

To incentivize last-minute backers, offer **limited-time rewards** or discounts. This could be a **flash sale** on a certain reward tier, exclusive access to a bonus, or special shout-outs to the last few backers.

Push for Media and Influencer Coverage

Try to secure some **final media coverage** or social media shout-outs during the last 24 hours of the campaign. The more visibility you can get in the final hours, the more likely you are to hit your goal.

Conclusion

Building momentum is essential to running a successful crowdfunding campaign. It involves creating buzz and anticipation long before your campaign goes live and continues through the entire lifecycle of the project.

Chapter 9: Managing Backer Expectations and Fulfillment

Setting Realistic Expectations from the Start

One of the biggest challenges in crowdfunding is ensuring that your backers' expectations are well-managed from the moment they decide to support your project, through the duration of your campaign, and all the way until fulfillment. Effective **communication** and **transparency** throughout the campaign process will help you maintain a good relationship with your backers, even when things don't go as planned.

You're asking people to trust you with their money and support a dream, so it's your responsibility to **manage that trust**. If you underpromise and overdeliver, you'll earn long-term backer loyalty. If you overpromise and underdeliver, you risk damaging your reputation and failing to meet your campaign's goals.

In this chapter, we'll look at how to manage backer expectations and fulfill your promises in a way that leaves everyone satisfied.

Communicating the Timeline

One of the first things you need to do on your crowdfunding page is set clear expectations around your **timeline**. Backers want to know when they will receive their rewards, and if the timeline changes, you need to communicate that **promptly**.

Be Transparent About Your Timeline

From the start, clearly outline your **estimated production and delivery dates**. While this can be a tricky area (especially if you're developing something new or working with manufacturers), being transparent from the beginning helps mitigate frustration later on.

Be conservative in your timeline estimates. It's better to promise a later delivery and deliver early than to promise an unrealistic timeline and miss it.
Include buffer time. Unexpected delays can happen—factoring in extra time for shipping,

manufacturing, or unforeseen issues gives you a cushion in case things don't go exactly as planned.

If delays do occur, **don't hide them**. Backers appreciate honesty, and keeping them updated regularly will show them that you are committed to transparency. Inform backers **early** if something goes off course, and offer them solutions or revised expectations.

Example of Timeline Transparency:

Initial Project Launch: June 1, 2024
Prototype Testing: July 2024
Manufacturing Begins: August 2024
Shipping/Delivery: October 2024
Late/Delayed Shipment Notice: Expected shipping delays due to factory challenges; we'll update with new shipping dates by September 2024.

By being realistic, your backers will be prepared for possible delays and will appreciate your proactive communication.

Providing Regular Updates

One of the most effective ways to manage expectations is by providing **consistent updates** throughout the duration of your campaign, and even after it ends. Keeping your backers informed about the project's progress, any issues that arise, and any exciting new developments will help them feel **involved** and **connected** to the process.

How to Provide Effective Updates:

Consistency: Set a schedule for when updates will go out. Whether it's once a week or bi-weekly, sticking to a predictable rhythm keeps your backers in the loop.

Transparency: Share the highs and lows. If you encounter a delay or obstacle, share it with backers. Provide details about what went wrong, how you're addressing it, and what the new timeline looks like.

Milestones: Celebrate when you reach key milestones—whether it's finishing prototyping, securing manufacturing, or shipping the first batch of products. This creates excitement and shows progress.

Behind-the-Scenes Content: Share photos, videos, or blog-style updates that show your work in progress, whether it's prototype testing, assembly, or packaging. Backers love being part of the **journey**.

Even if the news isn't always good, staying in regular communication will **build trust**. If your backers feel informed and included, they're much more likely to be patient and supportive.

Example of an Update:

"Dear Backers,

We're excited to announce that the first batch of prototypes is complete and on its way to us for testing! We're one step closer to manufacturing your rewards!

That said, we've encountered a slight delay in the production process due to an issue with one of our suppliers. We're working hard to resolve this and expect to ship by [new date]. We'll keep you updated every step of the way. Thank you for your continued support!"

Managing Backer Communication

Your backers are not just anonymous supporters—they're people who care about your project and will have questions, concerns, and feedback. Effective **communication** can turn potential conflicts into positive experiences.

Handling Questions and Concerns:

Be responsive: Always respond to messages and comments in a timely and courteous manner. If you don't have an answer to a question immediately, let the backer know you're looking into it and will get back to them.

Use FAQs: If you find that certain questions keep coming up (like shipping policies, rewards, or delivery dates), create a **Frequently Asked Questions** section on your campaign page or in your updates to save time and provide consistent answers.

Tone and Empathy: If backers express frustration or disappointment, always respond with empathy. Understand their concerns and show that you're doing everything possible to address the issue. A kind, professional tone can go a long way in smoothing over difficult situations.

Example of a Backer Concern Response:

"Hi [Backer Name],
Thanks so much for reaching out! We completely understand your concerns, and we're sorry for the inconvenience. Due to a delay with one of our suppliers, the delivery has been pushed back, but we're doing everything in our power to make sure your rewards are shipped as soon as possible. We'll be sure to keep you updated regularly with any changes. We appreciate your patience and support. Please don't hesitate to reach out with any other questions or concerns!"

Reward Fulfillment: The Final Step

The fulfillment stage of your crowdfunding campaign is the culmination of all your hard work—but it's also where many crowdfunding campaigns stumble. How you handle shipping, distribution, and reward fulfillment will have a direct impact on your reputation and your backers' overall experience.

Planning for Fulfillment:

Shipping Costs: Clearly communicate any shipping costs during the campaign and factor these into your reward tiers. Backers appreciate transparency about extra costs, such as international shipping or customs fees.

Logistics: Ensure that you have a solid logistics plan in place. Consider whether you'll handle fulfillment yourself or work with a fulfillment partner. If you're using a fulfillment service, do your due diligence to ensure they have a **track record** of success and can meet your timeline.

Backer Surveys: Use a **backer survey** (via platforms like BackerKit or CrowdOx) to collect essential information such as **shipping addresses**, size choices, or other personalization details. Send out the survey once your campaign ends, but be sure to follow up with any backers who don't respond.

Shipping Notifications: When orders are shipped, **send tracking numbers** to your backers. This helps them feel reassured that their rewards are on the way and gives them the ability to track the progress.

Handling Fulfillment Delays:

If fulfillment is delayed for any reason (whether due to production issues, shipping logistics, or customs delays), **communicate promptly** with backers and provide a clear new timeline. Keep them informed at every stage of the process to avoid frustration.

Example of a Fulfillment Update:

"Dear Backers,
We are thrilled to let you know that your rewards are on their way! Your packages have been shipped via [shipping service], and you should receive a tracking number in your inbox soon. Please allow 1-2 business days for the tracking to update.
Thank you for your support—we can't wait to hear what you think when your rewards arrive!
If you have any questions or concerns, please reach out, and we'll be happy to assist."

Post-Campaign Engagement

Even after the campaign is over and rewards have been fulfilled, your relationship with backers doesn't end. You can continue to build your brand and create future opportunities by **engaging with your community** long after the campaign has closed.

Ask for feedback: Once your backers receive their rewards, ask for their honest feedback. This will help you improve the product or process for future projects.

Stay in touch: Use your campaign's success as a springboard to continue building a community around your brand. Keep your backers engaged by sending updates, offering exclusive products, or launching new projects.

Share success stories: Share stories of how your project has impacted backers or the wider community, as well as any future plans you have for expanding your brand or creating new products.

Conclusion

Managing backer expectations and fulfillment is critical to the long-term success of your crowdfunding campaign. By setting realistic expectations, communicating transparently, and delivering on your promises, you'll not only gain the trust and support of your backers, but you'll also build a solid foundation for your brand's future growth.

The key to a successful campaign is clear and consistent communication—whether it's about delays, challenges, or successes. Always be honest, show appreciation for your backers, and be proactive in managing your rewards and logistics to ensure a smooth fulfillment process. By doing so, you'll set yourself up for ongoing success and create loyal backers who are eager to support your future endeavors.

Chapter 10: Leveraging Post-Campaign Strategies for Long-Term Success

The Power of Post-Campaign Engagement

While the primary goal of your crowdfunding campaign is to raise funds, a successful campaign should do far more than just reach its financial target—it should lay the groundwork for **sustained growth** and **long-term relationships** with your backers. Once your campaign ends and your rewards are shipped, the true potential of your crowdfunding efforts lies in how you choose to engage with your backers and how you leverage the momentum you've built.

In this chapter, we'll explore how to harness the post-campaign phase to build brand loyalty, create future opportunities, and ensure that the support you've gained doesn't fizzle out once the campaign concludes.

Express Gratitude and Acknowledge Your Backers

First and foremost, it's crucial to express your sincere **gratitude** to the people who made your campaign a success. Without your backers, none of this would have been possible. But gratitude goes beyond a quick "thank you" email; it's about creating a sense of community and showing your backers that their support truly matters to you.

Personalized Thank-Yous

A generic thank-you note is nice, but a personalized message makes your backers feel **valued** and **recognized**. Take the time to craft a heartfelt thank-you message that expresses not only your appreciation but also your excitement about the journey you've all been on together.

Direct messages: For major backers, those who pledged a significant amount, or influencers who helped spread the word, a direct, personalized message can go a long way. Thank them for their specific contribution, and let them know how integral they were to the success of the campaign.

Public acknowledgments: Use social media or updates to publicly acknowledge your backers, especially those who provided valuable support, feedback, or advice during the campaign. Consider creating a **"backer wall"** or "thank-you page" where you list the names of all contributors (with their consent).

Special Recognition and Rewards

For your most loyal backers or high-tier supporters, go above and beyond. A simple thank-you note may not be enough for those who helped shape the campaign. Consider sending **exclusive bonuses, personalized messages**, or even inviting them to be part of a private community that gets access to future updates or early releases.

Collect Feedback and Testimonials

Once the rewards are in the hands of your backers, it's time to ask for **feedback**—both on the product itself and the campaign process. Feedback provides you with valuable insights that can shape future versions of your product, improve your brand, and guide your next crowdfunding campaign.

Conduct Post-Campaign Surveys

While you may have sent out surveys during the campaign to collect shipping addresses or size preferences, now is the time to ask deeper questions about your backers' **experience**. A post-campaign survey is an effective way to gather data on:

Product satisfaction: How do backers feel about the product they received? Did it meet their expectations? Was the quality as promised? Are there any improvements they would suggest?
Campaign experience: How did they feel about the communication, the rewards, the fulfillment process?

Was there any part of the campaign that could have been improved?

Brand perception: How has your brand been perceived since the campaign ended? Do they see you as trustworthy and reliable? Would they recommend you to others?

Tools like **SurveyMonkey**, **Google Forms**, or **Typeform** can help you design a professional survey that gathers meaningful insights.

Gather Testimonials and User Reviews

Once you've received your feedback, consider asking satisfied backers to share **testimonials** or **reviews** that you can use in future marketing campaigns or on your website. A glowing testimonial from a backer who is genuinely excited about your product can help you build trust with future customers or potential investors.

Social media reviews: Ask backers to post about their experience on social media platforms like Instagram, Twitter, or TikTok, using hashtags that you've created for the campaign.

Video testimonials: If possible, request video testimonials where backers share their excitement about receiving your product. These can be incredibly powerful for social proof.

Example Feedback Request:

"Dear Backers,
We hope you're enjoying your [product]! As we work to improve and develop future products, we'd love to hear about your experience. What did you love? What can we improve? Please take a few minutes to fill out our quick survey [link], and as a thank-you, you'll be entered into a drawing for a special gift!"

Nurture Your Backer Community

A successful crowdfunding campaign doesn't end when the rewards are shipped—this is just the beginning of a deeper, ongoing relationship with your backers. They're not just one-time customers; they're your **brand ambassadors**, your **community**, and your **long-term supporters**. Keep them engaged and continue nurturing these relationships.

Create a Post-Campaign Email Sequence

If you've built an email list during your campaign (which you should have), don't let that list gather dust after the campaign ends. Create a post-campaign email sequence that provides:

Updates on your future plans, product releases, or expansions

Exclusive access to new products or rewards before they're available to the public

Behind-the-scenes content or insider information to make backers feel like they are part of your inner circle

Promotions or discounts on new products or services you're launching

In each email, maintain a **personal connection** with your backers by addressing them by name and letting them know how important their support is to you.

Example Post-Campaign Email:

"Dear [First Name],
We wanted to take a moment to thank you for being part of our campaign. Your support made this project possible, and we couldn't be more excited to have you on this journey with us.
We're already planning our next steps, and we want you to be the first to know. Check out our exclusive behind-the-scenes sneak peek at what's coming next [link to sneak peek].
Stay tuned, and thank you again for making this dream a reality!"

Create a Community Hub

Whether it's a **Facebook group, Discord server**, or a private section of your website, create a **community hub** where backers can connect with each other and with you. A strong community increases the likelihood that your backers will continue to support you in future campaigns, purchase additional products, and spread the word about your brand.

Facilitate discussions: Encourage backers to share their experiences with the product, suggest improvements, or share their creative uses of it.

Host Q&A sessions: Use the community to host live Q&A sessions, where backers can ask you about the project, future products, or anything they're curious about.

Example of a Community Engagement Invitation:

"Hey everyone,
We've just launched our **official backer community** on [Facebook/Discord]! This is the place to get all the latest updates, connect with other backers, share your feedback, and be part of the excitement as we work on future products. We'd love to have you join us!"

Leverage Your Campaign Success to Expand Your Brand

Your crowdfunding campaign likely attracted more than just backers—it may have attracted **media attention, influencers**, or **potential investors**. Don't let this initial attention go to waste. Use your post-campaign phase to build on the success of your campaign and expand your brand's reach.

Seek Media Coverage

After a successful campaign, reach out to journalists, bloggers, and media outlets that specialize in crowdfunding, startups, or your specific industry. Share your campaign's success story and how it has allowed you to grow your business. Many publications are interested in "success stories" from the crowdfunding world, and your campaign might make a compelling narrative.

Press releases: Draft a post-campaign press release detailing the success of the campaign, how it has affected your business, and any future goals you have. Be sure to highlight any new product launches, partnerships, or exciting developments.

Pitch to podcasts and influencers: Appearances on podcasts or interviews with influencers can help you expand your brand's reach. Share your journey with others to inspire potential customers or future backers.

Example Press Release:

"XYZ Company's crowdfunding campaign hits 200% of funding goal, paving the way for new product launches XYZ Company has exceeded its $100,000 funding goal on [Crowdfunding Platform], reaching 200% of the target and securing the future of its revolutionary [product]. With over [number] backers supporting the campaign, XYZ is now set to scale its operations and develop [additional products]."

Build a Brand That Lasts

The momentum you've built during your campaign can be leveraged into something much larger. Use the post-campaign phase to:

Expand your product line
Open an **online store** or **e-commerce site**
Offer **subscriptions**, **bundles**, or **limited-edition items**
Seek partnerships with other brands, distributors, or retailers to bring your product to new markets

Example Brand Expansion:

After successfully launching their first crowdfunding campaign for a smart home device, XYZ Company decides to expand into other home automation products, leveraging their existing backer community and media buzz to fund and market their new line.

Plan for Future Campaigns

A successful crowdfunding campaign is not just about raising funds for one project—it's about **building a long-term brand**.

Chapter 11: Scaling Your Crowdfunding Efforts: From One Campaign to a Thriving Brand

The Journey Beyond Your First Campaign

One of the most common mistakes that new creators make is viewing crowdfunding as a **one-off event**. After their initial campaign is successfully funded and the rewards are shipped, they may think their work is done—until they realize that true success lies in creating a **sustainable business model** that evolves over time. The crowdfunding campaign may have been the **starting point**, but it is just the beginning of your journey toward **scaling** and **growing** a lasting brand.

This chapter will walk you through strategies and tactics that will help you scale your efforts after a successful crowdfunding campaign, turning your single product into a thriving business and building a brand that will stand the test of time.

Understanding the Transition from Crowdfunding to E-commerce

Crowdfunding is often the **launchpad** for a new product, but once the campaign is over, you will need to transition your audience from **one-time backers** to **repeat customers**. You are no longer simply "funding" a product; you are now building an **e-commerce platform** where customers can return to buy again and again.

Set Up a Professional E-commerce Website

A successful crowdfunding campaign can attract attention and drive traffic, but this traffic needs to be converted into future sales. To do this, it is critical that you have an **e-commerce infrastructure** in place. Your website should do more than just serve as a place to collect orders—it should reflect the **values, mission**, and **aesthetic** of your brand.

User Experience (UX): Your website should be easy to navigate, with a clear call to action and smooth checkout process. Make it easy for visitors to find products, learn about your brand, and make a purchase.

Brand Storytelling: Use your website to tell the **story** of your brand and product. Connect with your audience on an emotional level by showing how your product is solving a problem or improving their lives. Include testimonials, high-quality images, and videos.

Product Pages: Ensure that your product pages are detailed and informative. Include product specifications, usage instructions, size guides (if applicable), and clear pricing. You should also feature **customer reviews** to build trust and social proof.

Integrate Payment and Shipping Solutions

A solid e-commerce platform also requires reliable **payment processing** and **shipping solutions**. Make sure you offer multiple payment methods (credit/debit cards, PayPal, Apple Pay, etc.) and have an efficient shipping system in place. For international customers, clearly outline any additional shipping fees or customs charges that may apply.

Example Transition from Crowdfunding to E-Commerce:

A company that successfully funded a smart kitchen appliance on Kickstarter moves to establish its own e-commerce website. They make the shift by integrating a Shopify store with seamless payment processing, offering free shipping on orders over a certain amount, and continuously updating the site with blog content, user-generated reviews, and cooking tips that align with their brand ethos.

Expanding Your Product Line to Build Brand Loyalty

Once your initial crowdfunding campaign is successful and you've established your online presence, it's time to think about **product expansion**. Building a **product line** that speaks to your backers' needs will keep them engaged and encourage **repeat purchases**.

Upsell and Cross-Sell Opportunities

Upselling involves offering a **premium version** of your product with additional features, customization options, or exclusive packaging.
Cross-selling suggests related products that complement the original item your backers bought. For example, if you funded a custom mug, you could cross-sell **coasters**, **mug warmers**, or **tea sets**.

These strategies not only increase your **average order value (AOV)** but also **enhance customer satisfaction** by providing backers with products that complement or enhance their original purchase.

Future Product Concepts Based on Feedback

As you gather feedback from your backers, you can start to develop new products that **solve other problems** or **meet additional needs** within your market. Consider launching products that expand upon your original concept but also appeal to a broader audience. For example:

If your original product was a **wearable device** for fitness, consider developing a **companion app** or **accessories** such as smart workout clothes or workout equipment.
If you funded a **home office accessory**, consider introducing related products like **ergonomic furniture** or **decor** to help create a complete workspace.

Remember to engage your existing backers and allow them to be a part of the development process. You could even offer **exclusive early access** to your new products in exchange for their loyalty and support.

Example of Product Line Expansion:

Your initial crowdfunding campaign was a success with a line of eco-friendly reusable water bottles. Following the campaign, you decide to introduce new products like **eco-friendly tote bags**, **portable straws**, and **bamboo cutlery sets**, expanding your brand into the eco-conscious lifestyle niche.

Building a Community of Loyal Brand Advocates

A thriving brand doesn't just rely on one-time purchases—it relies on creating a **community** of loyal customers and brand advocates. After your campaign, you need to continue **nurturing relationships** with your backers, turning them from **early supporters** into lifelong customers.

Create an Engaging Post-Campaign Community

Your backers were excited about your project during the campaign, but now that it's over, you need to keep that momentum going. A great way to do this is to **build a community** where your backers can continue to engage with your brand and each other.

Private Facebook Groups/Discord Channels: These platforms give your community a place to interact with your brand directly and with other customers who share their passion. It's also a great place to **solicit feedback** and keep backers engaged with future projects.
Exclusive Content: Provide your community with **early access, discounts,** or **behind-the-scenes content** that they can't get elsewhere. This makes your backers feel like **VIPs** and creates a sense of exclusivity.

Advocate-Driven Marketing

Encourage your loyal customers to share their experiences on social media and become **brand ambassadors**. People trust recommendations from their peers more than advertisements, so giving your backers the tools to advocate for your brand will create organic growth.

Referral Programs: Consider offering incentives for backers who refer new customers to your store. For example, you could give them a discount on future purchases or provide them with special rewards.

Social Media Campaigns: Create hashtags and social media campaigns where backers can share photos and videos of how they are using your product. Repost their content and show appreciation to help amplify your reach.

Example of Building Community:

A startup crowdfunding campaign for a sustainable fashion brand builds a private Facebook group where backers share their styling tips and photos of themselves wearing the brand's clothes. The company provides exclusive behind-the-scenes updates and discounts for active participants in the group. As a result, customers feel personally connected to the brand and are motivated to continue supporting it.

Utilizing Influencer Partnerships for Growth

After your crowdfunding campaign, you likely have the opportunity to expand your reach by working with **influencers** and **brand ambassadors** in your niche.

Influencers can help you reach new audiences and drive sales, especially if they are well-aligned with your brand values.

Identify the Right Influencers

Not all influencers are created equal. When considering partnerships, think about:

Niche relevance: An influencer in your product's niche (e.g., fitness, tech, eco-friendly living) is more likely to have an audience that will resonate with your product.
Engagement rates: Look for influencers who have a highly engaged audience, rather than just a high number of followers.
Authenticity: Influencers who are authentic and align with your values will deliver more credible and effective endorsements.

Collaborations and Co-Creation

Consider co-creating content with influencers to further **build trust** and **credibility**. Whether it's a YouTube review, Instagram post, or a collaborative product launch, co-creation makes your product feel more **organic** and **relatable**.

Example of Influencer Partnership:

After your campaign for a customizable planner, you partner with a well-known productivity YouTuber to create a limited edition version of the planner that she will promote to her followers. She shares honest reviews and provides exclusive discount codes for her audience, which leads to a surge in sales and brand exposure.

Funding and Financing Future Growth

With your e-commerce platform running and your customer base growing, the next step is to think about **scaling**. If your crowdfunding success has created a profitable business, you may be in a position to seek **additional funding** to take your brand to the next level.

Explore Traditional Funding Options

Angel Investors: Seek investors who are passionate about your industry and product. They can offer funding in exchange for equity, and in many cases, they bring valuable business experience and mentorship.

Venture Capital (VC): If you have a high-growth product and a clear plan for scaling, venture capital may be an option. Be mindful that VC funding often comes with expectations for rapid growth and profitability.

Bank Loans or Lines of Credit: Depending on your financial health, traditional loans may be a viable way to secure capital for expanding production, hiring staff, or marketing.

Chapter 12: Mastering Marketing Techniques for Post-Campaign Success

The Role of Marketing Beyond Crowdfunding

Once your crowdfunding campaign is successfully funded and the initial wave of excitement settles, you may feel a sense of accomplishment. However, it's important to remember that the true potential of your campaign lies not just in the funds you raised, but in how effectively you transition that momentum into **post-campaign marketing**. A successful crowdfunding campaign can catapult your brand into the public eye, but it's your **marketing strategies** that will ultimately determine whether that success continues to grow, plateau, or fade into obscurity.

In this chapter, we will explore the essential marketing techniques that can help you **sustain momentum** and ensure that your backers, and a new audience, continue to engage with your brand long after the campaign ends.

Crafting a Long-Term Brand Strategy

While crowdfunding provides an opportunity for a **one-off campaign**, it can also serve as the foundation for building a **long-term brand**. A successful

109

post-campaign marketing strategy should be centered around developing a **coherent brand identity** that continues to resonate with your audience and provides clear direction for your business growth.

Define Your Brand Values and Voice

The first step in crafting a long-term strategy is to define your brand's **core values**. These values should reflect what your brand stands for—whether it's **sustainability**, **innovation**, **quality craftsmanship**, or any other guiding principles. Be sure that these values are **consistent** across all marketing channels.

Your brand **voice** is equally important. The tone, language, and style with which you communicate with your customers must align with your brand values. Whether you choose to adopt a casual, friendly tone or a professional, authoritative voice, make sure it is **consistent** and **authentic**.

Brand Mission Statement: Create a statement that clearly outlines what your brand is about, why it exists, and how it will solve problems for your audience. This mission will guide your marketing efforts moving forward.

Example of Brand Mission:

"Our mission is to revolutionize personal health through innovative fitness technology that makes exercise easier and more accessible for people of all abilities."

Position Your Brand for the Long Term

Once you've defined your values and voice, position your brand to stand out in the long run. Think beyond your **product** and explore your brand's potential for **diversification**. Ask yourself:

How does your brand add value to people's lives beyond your current product?
Can you expand into new markets or demographics?
Can your brand evolve into something bigger than just a single product or service?

If your crowdfunding campaign was for a single product, think about how you can **expand** your offering over time. Introduce complementary products or **services** that align with your brand's mission and values.

Example of Brand Evolution:

A successful crowdfunding campaign for a sleek and functional backpack transitions into creating a full line of accessories, including laptop sleeves, duffle bags, and travel gear, all designed to complement the original product line and cater to the needs of busy professionals.

Content Marketing: Creating and Sharing Valuable Content

The post-campaign phase is the perfect time to embrace **content marketing** as a core part of your marketing strategy. Content marketing is not just about selling—it's about **educating, entertaining**, and **engaging** your audience in ways that provide value to them and keep them coming back.

Build an Engaging Content Strategy

Create a content plan that speaks to the needs, desires, and interests of your target audience. Your content should be **consistent, authentic**, and, most importantly, **valuable**. Focus on creating content that answers your audience's questions, provides solutions to their problems, and positions your brand as an **authority** in your niche.

Here are several types of content you should consider:

Blog posts: Regularly publish blog posts related to your product or industry. Share tips, tutorials, insights, or industry trends that resonate with your audience.

Blogging builds SEO (Search Engine Optimization) and drives organic traffic to your website.

Email newsletters: Keep your backers and subscribers informed about upcoming launches, company updates, or exclusive offers. Use newsletters to share personalized, value-added content.

How-to videos: Visual content, like tutorial videos, unboxing, and demonstrations, can significantly boost engagement. For a product-centric campaign, these videos help customers understand how to use the product and show off its features.

User-generated content (UGC): Encourage your customers to share their own content (pictures, reviews, videos) of them using your product. This form of social proof is incredibly valuable.

Example of Content Marketing:

A company that successfully funded a home gardening tool on Kickstarter starts a blog offering useful advice on urban gardening, composting, and organic farming. The brand becomes a trusted source of knowledge, and its blog traffic grows, leading to new product launches and repeat customers.

Repurpose Content Across Platforms

To maximize the value of your content, repurpose it across multiple platforms. For instance, a blog post can be turned into an infographic, a podcast episode, a social media post, or a video. This approach ensures that you reach a wider audience and maintain consistent messaging.

Example of Repurposing Content:

A "How to Use Our Product" blog post can be repurposed into a tutorial video for YouTube, snippets for Instagram stories, and a series of tweets sharing key insights.

Social Media Marketing: Building a Community Around Your Brand

Social media is an indispensable tool for post-campaign marketing. It's where your audience is spending a lot of their time, and it provides an avenue for **ongoing engagement**. If you haven't already, establish a presence across multiple social media platforms to reach different segments of your target audience.

Choose the Right Platforms

Not all social media platforms will be right for your brand. It's important to choose platforms where your **ideal customers** are most active. For example:

Instagram: Perfect for lifestyle brands, fashion, food, fitness, or anything visual. Instagram's features like

Stories, Reels, and IGTV offer multiple ways to engage with your audience.

Twitter: Great for quick updates, real-time engagement, and creating conversations around trending topics.

LinkedIn: Ideal for B2B brands, professional services, or businesses looking to connect with other companies or industry influencers.

TikTok: A fast-growing platform that is ideal for fun, viral content, and reaching younger demographics.

Engage with Your Community

Social media is about **two-way communication**. Don't just post your own content—engage with your followers, respond to comments, ask for feedback, and initiate conversations. Social media is an excellent platform for building **relationships** with your customers and encouraging a sense of **community**.

Host Q&A sessions: Go live and answer questions about your product, brand, or industry.

Run contests or giveaways: A great way to boost engagement and spread brand awareness. For example, run a giveaway where followers can win one of your products by tagging friends or sharing a post.

Behind-the-scenes content: Share the process behind your product development, packaging, or shipping to foster a more personal connection with your audience.

Example of Social Media Engagement:

A campaign that funded a fitness tracker regularly posts fitness tips on Instagram, while also running Q&A sessions and reposting user-generated content to build a loyal community.

Influencer Marketing: Leveraging Partnerships for Expanded Reach

Influencer marketing is a powerful way to expand your reach and build trust with potential customers. Collaborating with influencers, bloggers, and social media stars who have a following within your target market can help you boost your visibility and credibility.

Identify the Right Influencers

Before jumping into influencer partnerships, take the time to **vet** the influencers you want to work with. Look for influencers whose followers align with your target market. Assess the **engagement rate** (comments, likes, shares) of their posts rather than just their follower count. Authenticity is key.

Micro-Influencers vs. Macro-Influencers

Micro-Influencers (10k-100k followers) tend to have a **higher engagement rate** and often a more **dedicated** following. They can be more cost-effective and can help generate **quality leads**.

Macro-Influencers (100k+ followers) have a larger reach but often a more generalized audience. While expensive, they can significantly boost brand awareness.

Create Co-Branded Campaigns

For deeper partnerships, consider **co-creating** content with influencers, such as co-hosted events, custom products, or special collaborations. Co-branded campaigns not only expose your brand to a broader audience but also add **credibility** through the influencer's endorsement.

Example of Influencer Marketing:

A brand that successfully funded a smart kitchen gadget collaborates with a well-known chef on Instagram to create a series of cooking videos using their product. The chef's followers trust their expertise, and as a result, product sales soar.

Paid Advertising: Amplifying Your Reach

While organic marketing efforts can take time to yield results, **paid advertising** can help you accelerate your brand growth and reach new customers more quickly. Running ads across various channels like **Facebook**, **Instagram**, **Google**, or **YouTube** allows you to target specific demographics and re-engage past customers.

Retargeting Ads

Retargeting ads are a powerful tool for reconnecting with people who have previously shown interest in your product but didn't complete a purchase.

Chapter 13: Leveraging Customer Feedback to Fuel Product Development and Growth

The Power of Customer Feedback in the Post-Campaign Phase

After your crowdfunding campaign wraps up, the excitement of reaching your funding goal can be exhilarating. However, once your product hits the hands of backers, you enter a new phase: the critical post-launch phase. This is where the **real learning** begins. Your customers will provide invaluable **feedback** that can shape the future of your brand. By listening closely to their voices, you can refine your products, improve customer satisfaction, and fuel **long-term growth**.

In this chapter, we will explore strategies for **gathering**, **analyzing**, and **acting upon customer feedback** to build a better product and create a stronger brand.

Collecting Customer Feedback

The first step toward leveraging customer feedback is to establish clear methods for **collecting** it. You want to ensure that you capture feedback from a variety of sources and at different points in the customer journey.

Surveys and Questionnaires

One of the most effective ways to gather detailed feedback from your customers is by sending out **surveys**. After customers receive their products, consider sending a **post-purchase survey** to gather insights on their experience.

Product Satisfaction: Questions like "How satisfied are you with your purchase?" or "Was the product as described?" can help you assess if your product met expectations.
Customer Experience: Ask about the overall experience with your campaign and shipping. Did they feel well-informed? Were there any pain points?
Feature Requests: Solicit feedback on any features or improvements they'd like to see in future iterations of the product.

There are several online tools, such as **SurveyMonkey**, **Google Forms**, or **Typeform**, that allow you to easily create and send surveys to your customers.

Post-Delivery Communication

Once your backers receive their products, don't let the communication stop there. A **follow-up email** a few days or weeks after delivery is a great way to check in and request feedback. You can ask questions like:

"How has your experience been with our product so far?"
"Is there anything we could have done better?"
"Would you recommend this product to others?"

Follow-ups also give you the opportunity to address any potential **issues** quickly, which can help you **maintain positive relationships** with your customers.

Social Media Listening

Social media provides a wealth of real-time feedback from customers. By actively monitoring platforms like **Instagram**, **Twitter**, and **Facebook**, you can gain insights into how people are perceiving your product.

Hashtags: Encourage customers to use specific hashtags when posting about your product. You can easily track and analyze these posts.
Mentions: Monitor direct mentions of your brand or product name to see what people are saying.
Reviews: Pay attention to customer reviews on social media, your website, and third-party review platforms. Reviews are a goldmine for honest feedback.

Example of Customer Feedback Collection:

A company that funded a smart speaker via crowdfunding uses a combination of email follow-ups, social media monitoring, and surveys to collect feedback. They notice that many customers are asking for integration with a specific music streaming service, which was not originally included. They prioritize this feature in their next product update.

Analyzing Customer Feedback

Once you've collected customer feedback, the next step is to **analyze** it. At this stage, it's essential to look for both **quantitative** and **qualitative** data to get a comprehensive understanding of your product's performance and how customers perceive it.

Categorize Feedback

It's important to categorize the feedback you receive so you can spot **patterns** and **trends**. Consider grouping feedback into the following categories:

Product performance: Does the product work as advertised? Are there any functional issues or common complaints?

Ease of use: Are customers able to use the product as intended without confusion? Are there instructions that need clarification?

Design and aesthetics: Are people happy with the look and feel of the product? Is the design user-friendly?

Customer service and delivery: How satisfied are customers with the purchasing and shipping process? Were there delays or issues?

Future features: What additional features or improvements do customers want to see in future versions?

Quantitative vs. Qualitative Feedback

Quantitative data refers to measurable feedback, such as survey ratings (e.g., "rate your satisfaction from 1 to 10"). This type of data can give you clear, numeric insights into customer satisfaction.

Qualitative data refers to more subjective feedback, such as comments and reviews. While harder to measure, qualitative feedback is often where you'll find **detailed suggestions**, **emotions**, and **specific concerns**.

For example, a customer might give you a rating of "8/10" for product satisfaction (quantitative), but in the open-ended comments, they might mention that the product could use a "better grip for easier handling" (qualitative).

Tools for Analyzing Feedback

There are several tools available to help you aggregate and analyze customer feedback:

Google Analytics: You can track behavior on your website (such as page views, bounce rates, etc.) to understand how users are interacting with your content.
Sentiment Analysis: Tools like **MonkeyLearn** or **Lexalytics** can analyze social media and customer reviews to identify the general sentiment (positive, negative, neutral) of customer feedback.
Customer Support Software: Platforms like **Zendesk** or **Freshdesk** provide ticketing systems where customer inquiries can be logged and analyzed for recurring themes.

Example of Analyzing Feedback:

After analyzing several surveys and reviews, you notice that 30% of users mention they are having trouble setting up the product, while others are praising the product's functionality. This gives you a clear indication that the setup process could use simplification, and you can start addressing this in the next version or through updated documentation.

Acting on Customer Feedback

The real value of customer feedback comes when you take **action** based on it. If you ignore or fail to address common issues, your customers may feel unheard, and you risk **losing trust**.

Iterating on Product Design

Customer feedback is an essential tool for **product development**. By iterating on your product based on real-world usage and user suggestions, you can improve it over time.

Fix bugs and functional issues: If customers consistently report functional problems, prioritize fixing them. This can be particularly important for tech-related products or anything that requires complex setup.

Enhance features: If your customers are asking for new features, assess whether they align with your overall product vision and brand values. Adding new features can improve your product's usefulness and appeal.

Design improvements: If there are common complaints about the product's design or user experience, work with your team to make improvements. For example, adjusting the product's shape for better ergonomics or redesigning packaging to be more environmentally friendly.

Example of Acting on Feedback:

A tech gadget company receives feedback that users struggle with syncing their device to their phone. After collecting data and customer input, they develop a software update to improve the sync process, then notify customers via email and app notifications about the fix.

Updating Marketing and Messaging

Sometimes feedback can reveal valuable insights into how customers perceive your brand and product, which can be used to refine your marketing messages. If customers often mention specific product features they love or talk about how the product benefits them, you can use this feedback to craft more targeted and compelling **marketing content**.

For example, if users frequently mention that your product has **saved them time**, you could use this as a central theme in your marketing messaging, highlighting the time-saving benefits in your ads, emails, and social media campaigns.

Example of Adjusting Marketing:

After hearing from multiple backers that they love the **simplicity** of your product, you adjust your marketing language to emphasize ease of use. You use testimonials that highlight how the product simplifies users' lives, leading to better conversion rates and engagement.

Creating a Feedback Loop: Building Ongoing Relationships

The process of gathering feedback should not be a one-time event. A **feedback loop** is a continual process that ensures you're always listening to your customers, evolving your product, and improving the customer experience.

Engage Customers in Product Development

Encourage customers to be **co-creators** of your product development. You can involve them in the process in several ways:

Beta Testing: Before launching major product updates, invite your most loyal customers to participate in **beta testing**. Their early feedback can help you fix issues before the public release.

Focus Groups: Conduct focus groups to dive deeper into customer preferences and pain points. This can provide qualitative insights that surveys might miss.

Crowdsourced Features: Let customers vote on or suggest features they'd like to see in future updates. This gives them a sense of **ownership** in the brand's evolution.

Build a Long-Term Relationship with Feedback Channels

Keep your feedback channels open and ensure that your customers feel like their opinions are being valued. Respond to comments on social media, address complaints promptly, and highlight any changes or improvements that were made based on their feedback. This will build trust and loyalty, turning customers into **advocates**.

Example of Ongoing Feedback Loop:

A company that created a smartwatch invites backers to become part of an exclusive **user feedback panel**. They continuously send product updates and ask for input on new features, ensuring customers feel engaged in the evolution of the product.

Chapter 14: Scaling Your Brand After a Successful Campaign

The Opportunity for Growth: Taking Your Brand to the Next Level

Congratulations—your crowdfunding campaign was a success, and you've now built a product that has garnered significant attention from customers and backers. While raising funds and fulfilling orders is a major milestone, it's only the beginning of your journey. Now comes the challenging and rewarding phase of **scaling your brand.**

Scaling a brand isn't just about increasing sales or expanding operations; it's about creating a sustainable, thriving business that can grow without losing sight of the core values and customer satisfaction that made your campaign successful. In this chapter, we will explore strategies for taking your brand to new heights—building on the momentum of your campaign to achieve long-term success.

Expanding Your Product Line

One of the most straightforward ways to scale your brand is to expand your product offering. When done thoughtfully, a **diversified product line** can open up new revenue streams, attract different customer segments, and increase the lifetime value of your customers.

Identify Opportunities for Product Expansion

Building on your initial product, consider how you can introduce **complementary products** that naturally fit into your brand's ecosystem. Your existing customers are often the best source of insights when it comes to future product development. After gathering feedback, look for recurring themes or requests for additional features or entirely new products.

Accessory Lines: If your initial product was a tech gadget, you could create accessories that enhance its functionality, such as carrying cases, charging stations, or new software add-ons.

Upgrades or Variants: Create premium versions or updated models with additional features. For example, if you've launched a fitness tracker, you might release a new version with advanced health metrics or improved design.

Bundling: Offer product bundles that include your original product and new accessories at a discounted price. Bundles encourage customers to purchase more items while increasing average order value.

Example of Product Line Expansion:

A company that launched a portable speaker successfully in their crowdfunding campaign later introduced a series of audio accessories, including headphones, portable chargers, and Bluetooth adapters, catering to the same audience and increasing revenue.

Create Product Development Roadmaps

As you look to expand, develop a clear **product roadmap** that outlines the timeline, resources, and strategies needed to bring new products to market. Be sure to align these new products with your brand's core mission and values. You don't want to flood the market with too many unrelated products; instead, each new offering should contribute to your brand's larger narrative and customer promise.

Expanding Your Market Reach

Your crowdfunding campaign likely attracted an audience that already aligns with your brand's mission, but as you scale, you'll want to target **new markets** to continue growing. Here are some strategies for expanding your reach:

Geographic Expansion

One of the most effective ways to scale is by targeting new **geographies**. If your crowdfunding campaign was primarily focused on a local or national market, consider expanding internationally or regionally. This requires careful research, but it opens up vast opportunities.

International Shipping: If you haven't already, consider offering international shipping. Many successful crowdfunding projects that initially focused on domestic markets have expanded globally by partnering with international fulfillment centers.

Localized Marketing: Customize your marketing messages and advertisements for each new market, tailoring the language, imagery, and cultural references to resonate with local customers.

New Demographics

While your crowdfunding campaign likely targeted a specific group of backers, scaling your brand means reaching **new customer segments**. This could mean appealing to new age groups, income brackets, or interests. For example, if your product was initially designed for tech enthusiasts, you may want to target **mainstream consumers** who are looking for everyday solutions.

Influencer Partnerships: Collaborate with influencers in different niches to reach new customer segments. For instance, if your fitness tech product did well with young professionals, an influencer in the wellness or parenting space may help you reach families or older adults.

Advertising: Use **paid advertising** on platforms like Facebook, Google, and Instagram to create segmented ads that appeal to different demographics.

Example of Market Expansion:

A company that crowdfunded a sustainable travel bag for eco-conscious travelers begins selling their product in international markets, partnering with local eco-friendly influencers to help promote the product across Europe and Asia. They tailor their messaging to fit each region's unique sustainability challenges and preferences.

Building a Scalable Marketing Strategy

As your brand grows, you'll need to implement a **scalable marketing strategy** to keep up with demand while maintaining the quality of your customer interactions. Here are some key tactics to consider as you scale your marketing efforts:

Automate and Streamline Marketing Efforts

When scaling your marketing strategy, it's essential to implement **automation** tools that allow you to reach more customers without sacrificing personalization. Here are some tools and tactics to consider:

Email Marketing Automation: Use platforms like **Mailchimp**, **Klaviyo**, or **ActiveCampaign** to send targeted, automated email campaigns to segmented lists. Whether it's for welcome emails, abandoned cart reminders, or post-purchase follow-ups, automation ensures timely communication at scale.
CRM Software: A **Customer Relationship Management (CRM)** system like **HubSpot** or **Salesforce** will help you manage customer interactions across multiple touchpoints and ensure that your marketing efforts are streamlined and effective.
Social Media Scheduling: Use platforms like **Hootsuite**, **Buffer**, or **Sprout Social** to schedule and manage social media posts in advance. This can free up your time while maintaining consistent engagement with your audience.

Leverage User-Generated Content

As your brand scales, one of the most powerful marketing tools you can leverage is **user-generated content (UGC)**. Your customers and backers can become your best advocates by posting their experiences with your products on social media. Encourage them to share their stories by offering incentives like discounts, features on your official social media channels, or even rewards for the best content.

Hashtag Campaigns: Create a branded hashtag and encourage users to post content using that hashtag. This could be as simple as sharing a picture of them using your product or telling a story about how it has impacted their life.

Customer Testimonials: Collect and share **testimonials** from satisfied customers to build social proof. Customer reviews, video testimonials, or stories on social media can significantly increase your credibility.

Example of Scalable Marketing:

A sustainable home goods company creates a referral program where existing customers get discounts for referring friends and family. The company uses email marketing automation to send personalized referral links and reminders, scaling the program effectively.

Building a Strong Team and Operations Infrastructure

As your brand scales, it's critical to invest in building a team and operational infrastructure that can support increased demand. Here's how to prepare for growth:

Hire the Right Talent

To scale successfully, you need to build a team that can support your vision. Whether it's in marketing, customer support, operations, or product development, your team should be aligned with your brand values and equipped with the necessary skills to handle the growing demands of the business.

Core Team: Identify key roles within your organization—such as marketing manager, customer support lead, or product development specialist—and hire professionals who can handle specific aspects of your business.

Outsource: If you can't yet afford to hire full-time employees for every role, consider outsourcing certain functions to third-party agencies or freelancers. For example, you might want to outsource **graphic design,**

social media management, or **content creation** to professionals while keeping core functions in-house.

Scale Your Operations

As demand for your product grows, you'll need to scale your operational infrastructure to ensure timely fulfillment and customer satisfaction. This could mean:

Inventory Management: Invest in **inventory management systems** like **TradeGecko** or **Cin7** to monitor stock levels, automate ordering, and ensure you're never out of stock.

Fulfillment: Consider partnering with a third-party logistics (3PL) provider for warehousing and order fulfillment. This can help you handle shipping more efficiently as you scale, especially if you're moving into international markets.

Example of Team and Operations Scaling:

A small startup that initially fulfilled orders in-house partners with a 3PL service to handle an influx of orders after scaling. They hire a logistics manager to ensure everything runs smoothly and also expand their customer service team to respond to increased inquiries.

Protecting Your Brand and Intellectual Property

137

As your brand grows, it becomes increasingly important to protect your intellectual property (IP) and ensure your brand's reputation is safeguarded. Here are a few steps to take:

Trademark Your Brand

Ensure that your **brand name**, **logo**, and any unique product names or slogans are **trademarked**. This helps protect your intellectual property and prevents others from copying your brand.

Patents: If your product involves any unique design or functionality, consider applying for a **patent** to protect it from being copied.

Copyrights: Protect any original creative content, like product designs, marketing materials, or website content, by registering copyrights.

Brand Reputation Management

As your brand grows, there will be more people talking about it—both positive and negative. **Monitor your brand reputation** through tools like **Google Alerts** or **Mention** to ensure that your brand's online presence remains strong and consistent.

Respond to Negative Reviews: Address customer concerns quickly and professionally, and work to resolve any issues that arise.

Build Strong Relationships: Maintaining excellent customer service and building a community of loyal customers will go a long way in preventing negative feedback.

Chapter 15: Building a Community Around Your Brand

The Importance of Community for Long-Term Success

In today's marketplace, successful brands don't just sell products—they build **communities**. A community is more than just a group of customers; it's a loyal, engaged network of people who believe in your mission, support your vision, and help spread the word about your brand. Building a strong community around your product or service is crucial for long-term success, as it creates a foundation for **brand loyalty**, **word-of-mouth marketing**, and **sustained growth**.

In this chapter, we will explore how to **cultivate a community** that is not just buying from you, but actively **engaging with your brand** and contributing to its success.

Defining Your Community's Values and Purpose

The first step in building a community is to define what your brand stands for. Your customers should know what your brand represents, what it believes in, and what values it holds. These values will guide the tone, culture, and activities of your community.

Identify Core Brand Values

Think about what makes your brand **different** from others and why people chose to support you in the first place. Is your brand built around sustainability, innovation, creativity, or social impact? These are the foundations for the community you want to build.

Authenticity: Community members are looking for brands that are real and transparent. Ensure your values and messaging align with your actions.

Purpose: Beyond just selling a product, what problem are you solving, and how does that contribute to the lives of your customers or to society at large? People are more likely to invest time, energy, and resources into communities that have a clear and compelling purpose.

Example of Core Brand Values:

If your brand focuses on **eco-conscious living**, then your community's values may include sustainability, environmental activism, and social responsibility. You could organize clean-up events, share eco-friendly tips, or highlight environmental issues, giving your community a purpose that transcends product ownership.

Creating Spaces for Engagement

To build a community, you need to create **spaces** where people can connect, interact, and engage with your brand and each other. Whether online or offline, these spaces serve as a home for your brand's community and are essential for fostering connections.

Online Communities

In today's digital world, creating an **online community** is often the most effective way to connect with a large group of people. Here are a few platforms you can use:

Social Media Groups: Create private groups on Facebook, LinkedIn, or even Reddit where your customers can engage with each other. These spaces can be used for product discussions, support, and sharing experiences.

Branded Forums: Set up a forum or community space on your website using tools like **Discourse**, **Vanilla Forums**, or **Tribe**. A branded forum gives your community a dedicated space for conversation and content.

Slack/Discord Channels: Many brands are turning to apps like Slack or Discord to create more dynamic, real-time communities. These platforms can be set up for specific topics like product feedback, fan art, behind-the-scenes updates, or even casual socializing.

In-Person Events and Meetups

While online spaces are essential, don't overlook the power of **in-person engagement**. Events such as meetups, product launches, pop-up shops, or workshops allow you to connect with your community face-to-face.

Brand Experiences: Organize events where customers can experience your products in person, meet the team behind the brand, and network with other like-minded individuals.

Conferences and Conventions: Attend or sponsor industry events where you can meet potential customers and other brands, or even create your own branded events that allow people to learn more about your products in an immersive setting.

Example of Online and Offline Engagement:

A fitness brand that launched through crowdfunding creates a **Facebook Group** for customers to share workout tips, recipes, and success stories. They also organize annual **community fitness meetups** in major cities to strengthen the bond between members and the brand.

Empowering Your Community Members

For a community to thrive, your customers should feel **empowered** and encouraged to contribute, share, and engage. Empowering your community means giving them a sense of **ownership** and **purpose**, and making them feel like they are an integral part of your brand's journey.

Encourage User-Generated Content (UGC)

User-generated content is an incredible way to increase community involvement. When customers create content—whether it's product reviews, social media posts, videos, or blogs—they're not just engaging with your brand; they're also sharing your story with their own networks.

Hashtags: Create a unique hashtag that encourages your community to share their experiences with your brand. The hashtag can be specific to a product or event, like #MyBrandStory or #BrandNameAdventures.
Contests and Challenges: Host fun challenges or giveaways that incentivize UGC. For instance, encourage customers to share a photo of them using your product with a chance to win exclusive prizes.

Highlight Community Leaders

Identify **community leaders**—passionate individuals who consistently engage with your brand and take an active role in conversations. These individuals can help moderate your community spaces, offer feedback, or even become **brand ambassadors**. Recognizing their efforts can further strengthen their loyalty and engagement.

Featured Members: Regularly feature standout members of your community on social media or in newsletters. It shows appreciation and motivates others to contribute.

Ambassador Programs: Create a program that rewards loyal community members who spread the word about your brand. Offer exclusive perks, early access to new products, or financial rewards for successful referrals.

Example of Empowering the Community:

A photography brand encourages users to share their photos on Instagram using their product hashtag. Each month, they feature one "photo of the month" on their website and social media channels, providing the winner with a discount and free product. This boosts engagement and gives customers the chance to showcase their creativity.

Providing Value Beyond Products

For your community to remain loyal and active, you must offer **value beyond just selling products**. Building a community means creating a space where people feel they are gaining something more than just a transaction.

Educational Content

Offer **free educational content** that aligns with your community's interests and needs. By positioning your brand as an expert in the field, you can build trust and long-term loyalty.

How-To Guides and Tutorials: Create resources that help your community get more out of your product. If you sell tech gadgets, for example, you might offer guides on how to maximize functionality or troubleshoot common issues.

Webinars and Workshops: Host live sessions where your community can interact with experts, ask questions, and learn something new. This could be a fitness brand offering workout plans or a cooking brand hosting a cooking class.

Exclusive Content and Perks

Reward your community members with exclusive content, early access to new products, or members-only discounts. This adds value to their engagement and gives them a reason to remain active.

Member-Only Newsletters: Offer insider information, sneak peeks, or behind-the-scenes updates that are exclusive to your community members.

Early Access: Let your community know about new product releases or promotions before they are available to the general public. This makes them feel special and reinforces their loyalty.

Example of Providing Value:

A health and wellness brand builds a dedicated **online learning center** with educational resources on fitness, nutrition, and mental health. Community members have access to free workshops, expert advice, and downloadable guides, creating more value than just purchasing a product.

Recognizing and Rewarding Loyalty

As your community grows, it's essential to **reward** and **recognize** your most loyal customers. By showing appreciation, you build stronger relationships and encourage continued engagement.

Loyalty Programs

Implement a **loyalty program** where members earn rewards for engaging with your brand. Rewards could include points for purchases, social media shares, or event participation. Over time, these points can be redeemed for discounts, exclusive content, or special offers.

Tiered Rewards: Create a tiered loyalty system where the more a member engages, the better the rewards. For example, a customer who shares about your brand on social media may earn more rewards than one who only buys from you.

Celebrate Milestones

Celebrate milestones such as anniversaries, product launches, or reaching a certain number of community members. Acknowledging these achievements shows your community that they are part of something significant.

Customer Spotlights: Regularly highlight loyal customers who have contributed to the community, whether through content creation, feedback, or simply being an advocate for your brand.

Anniversary Celebrations: Celebrate the anniversary of your campaign or product launch by offering special discounts or hosting a community event.

Example of Rewarding Loyalty:

A cosmetics brand uses a points-based loyalty program where customers can earn points for every purchase and social media share. Members who reach a certain point threshold are given VIP access to new product launches, free products, and exclusive events.

Listening and Evolving with Your Community

A successful community is a **two-way relationship**—you must listen to your community's feedback, address their concerns, and evolve based on their needs. Regularly engage with your members, ask for feedback, and show them that their voices matter.

Surveys and Feedback Loops

Create regular **feedback loops** through surveys or open-ended questions where community members can share their thoughts on product improvements, new features, or even how to improve the community itself.